Helping Students Revise Their Writing

PRACTICAL STRATEGIES, MODELS, AND MINI-LESSONS THAT MOTIVATE STUDENTS TO BECOME BETTER WRITERS

by Marianne Tully, Ed.D.

SCHOLASTIC
PROFESSIONAL BOOKS

NEW YORK • TORONTO • LONDON • AUCKLAND • SYDNEY

DEDICATION

*To the children and teachers of South Orangetown Schools,
Rockland County, New York.*

Cover design by Vincent Ceci and Jaime Lucero
Interior design by Solutions by Design, Inc.
Interior illustration by Marika Hahn

ISBN 0-590-86565-X

Table of Contents

Acknowledgments

I applaud the work that the teachers and administrators of South Orangetown Central Schools have been doing in helping our students to grow as writers. I am especially grateful to the many excellent teachers with whom I work at William O. Schaefer School in Tappan, New York. They inspire me with their long hours of preparation for their teaching and with their good energy, humor, and dedication. Among them I want to mention those who contributed photos and whose students contributed writing samples to this book: Mary Danner, Eileen Griffith, Anne O'Brien, Lynette Pantale, Marie Pettee, Donna Schaefer, Shelley Stern, Eileen Stout, Pat Mulcahy, Ellen Brown, Vickie Wu Zazwczny, Joan Rudolph, and Pat Wolleben. Christine Marchese, who is now a teacher in North Rockland, was also generous with her ideas.

I also thank those teachers in our other district schools who are doing exciting things with their students in writing. I asked a few of these teachers for student writing samples, photos, and ideas and they deserve mention for the time and attention it took: Kottie Christie-Blick and Eileen Miranda of the Cottage Lane School and Julie Cremeans and Rose Nappi of the South Orangetown Middle School. Thanks to the principals of each of those schools for their support: Robert Hendrickson and Emmanuel Kostakis, respectively.

The students who contributed their writing samples to this book are the following:
James Rondina, Susan Kim, Josh Drago, Lexi Lampel, Stephanie Graff, Danny DiLoreto, Maggie Gordon-Fogelson, Nick Stefos, Tom Philip, Perri Gerard-Little, Anella Bokhari, Katie Breder, David Jones, Justin Grimm-Greenblatt, Stephen Champon, Katie Hobday, Jonathan Hernandez, Sophia Hoffman, and Casey Sullivan. I am grateful to them for their cooperation and for their excellent writing.

Thanks to the following students who appear in photos in this book:
Sonya Harum, Sally Breer, Amanda Eng-Godburn, Fiona Gibney, Lauren Rosko, Lexi Lampel, Matthew Nugent, Sarah Garland, Clarisa Yanga, Julia Naddeo, Patrick Casey, Paula Fugazzotto, David Merck, Michael Fossner, Amy Croyle, Ross Springsteen, Brian Delaney, Allison O'Connor, Bobby Vugiukas, Erick Adrien, Alexandra Gable, Jaclyn Hackett, Jane Kallukalam, Anella Bokhari, Caitlin Nugent, Howard Ng, George Garrecht, Danielle Descarfino, Craig Coombs, Luis Maturo, Alyssa Glasser, Stephanie Kuhn, Jonathan Ostrowsky, Justin Kopunek, Amanda Weiss, Adeoluwa Kolade, Diane Bruen, Shane Williams, Ted Plenge.

I also acknowledge the encouragement of the superintendent of our school district, Dr. Morton Sherman. He supported my doing demonstration lessons on writing in my school and encouraged our teachers to move forward with process writing.

This project got its start and was nurtured by a former colleague of mine, Dr. Susan Shafer, with whom I had taught ten years ago in New York City. Susan, a writer herself, scouted out ideas from Lucy Calkins' writing workshop program in the early to mid-eighties and implemented them in her classroom. She then shared them with me.

Finally, I acknowledge the strong support of someone who loves words, my husband, Sigmund Hack.

Preface

This book grew from my experiences as a classroom teacher and as a person who works with classroom teachers. I am the principal of an elementary school of 400 students in a suburban community north of New York City.

Before I became a principal, I used a writing-process approach for six years with my classes of third graders in a school on the upper west side of Manhattan. I have shared with my teachers the way that I actually taught writing to my own students. Through in-school workshops and demonstration lessons in the classroom, I was able to show my teachers the strategies that have worked for me. We have fine teachers in my school and they have, in turn, helped me expand my ideas. They have done this through discussions, observations, ongoing work with students, selected reading, conferences on writing instruction, and our K–12 teacher-led writing portfolio study group.

The focus of the book arose from the fact that revising is the hardest part of the process for the kids to do and for the teachers to teach. As a principal, I wanted to be able to help teachers with this, and I knew that there was very little written on the topic. I was aware that over the last ten to fifteen years, teachers in general had been successful in getting their students to write fluently. The frustrating part of the process had been to get students to revise their writing. The writers' conference gives feedback to the writer, but it is very hard for children to take that feedback and go back to their desks and actually add what needs to be added and change what needs to be changed. I wanted to write a book that offers practical strategies to effectively motivate students and to help them build the skills to revise their own work.

My method in writing this book was to sift through ideas, brainstorm, try things out, think through problems, and make the strategies clear. I have generally used pieces of personal-experience writing to illustrate the strategies because it is the type through which children of this age can find their most distinctive voice.

All of this has helped to shape the book that follows.

*I*ntroduction

Revision is a part of writing.
> —Strunk and White, *The Elements of Style*

*N*o, I like it the way it is," second-grader Nick responded when I suggested that he include a detail explaining Green Day for those not familiar with punk rock groups. He and I were modeling a writers' conference before his teacher and his classmates. The strength of his refusal to revise was impressive. Here I was, the school principal, making a suggestion before an

audience of his teacher and his peers, and he wasn't budging. He just didn't want to revise. This is not so unusual. Most students are generally pleased with their first draft and don't see the point of working on it further. This leaves us, as educators, with the question: If we want children to own their writing, should we insist that they refine it?

Answering this question isn't easy. We respect our students' instincts about their writing and worry that if we intervene in the process, some children will get the message that their writing isn't good enough and will stop writing. Some teachers of writing have even come to the conclusion that most elementary school children are just not developmentally ready to revise their work. In her book *Literacy at the Crossroads*, noted educator Regie Routman says, "There's no incentive for a student to revise unless the writing is for a purpose the student chooses and/or values . . . . Be realistic about revision. Don't expect kindergarten and first-grade children to do much revision. The act of writing and transcription is challenge enough."

While there are no easy answers when it comes to teaching writing, I believe children in grades two and above can handle revision if they are taught the skills that enable them to do it and if revision is presented to them as process of developing—rather than correcting—writing. Kids have to know that it's not about fixing errors, but about making their meaning clear. And we teachers have to see the process of revision as an answer to the question: "How can I help my students to grow as writers?" As Donald Murray says in *Shoptalk: Learning to Write with Writers*, writing *is* rewriting; if we accept a student's first draft as is, the child misses out on the heart of the writing process. He or she misses the opportunity to extend the piece and make it even better, and also misses the chance to grow as a writer and a thinker.

The goal of this book is to help you set up in the classroom conditions that get children to write fluently, reread what they've written, think about it, ask questions about it, compare it to models of good writing, and then use these new perspectives to revisit and rework the piece. *Revision* means "to look at again." Children grow as writers when they experience themselves as active revisers and shapers of their writing.

CHAPTER 1

The Writing Process: An Overview

The essence of writing is rewriting.
 —William Zinsser, in *Writers at Work*

What Writing Is

*W*hat is writing? Why do kids have to learn so many kinds of writing? Why can't they just learn to write their sentences and paragraphs properly and do their assignments? These are questions that parents often ask me. To be clear for ourselves, our students, and their parents, it's helpful to consider just what writing *is*. Writing is many things, each of which goes to the heart of what a good education is all about. Writing is a way of learning, not just a tool to record what one already knows. Writing is a way of discovering and constructing meaning. Writing is a way of thinking. Writing is a way of raising consciousness—both in the writer and in the reader. Writing is central to the educative process. Every good teacher knows this.

Over the last ten to twenty years, various approaches to teaching writing have been used, celebrated, modified, and rejected—and usually in that order! Some of the best are still flourishing and evolving. I think it's fair to say that the constant in all current writing programs—from cutting-edge university models to commercial textbooks—is an awareness that children don't learn to write by the traditional model, that is, by writing according to the teacher's specifications, handing the piece in, and getting a corrected version back with a grade. Students learn to write by doing the same things that the adult writer does, including choosing a topic, writing a draft, sharing and getting feedback, revising, and publishing. This is called the writing process. The writing process is expressed in various ways. I like the following simple schema:

- ✽ PREWRITE

- ✽ WRITE

- ✽ REWRITE

Below you will find some starter strategies for each step. Many more writing strategies—from producing initial drafts to final edits—are discussed in later chapters.

Fifth graders work on their first drafts.

Prewriting Strategies

Thinking

This is the most important thing to do as one writes, not only in the beginning of the process but throughout the work. Before having students write about a personal experience, ask them: "Think about what is important to you, what you've done, or what has happened to you. Think about why you want to write on this topic. Think about who your audience will be."

Making Lists

Lists help writers to get their ideas down quickly and begin to discover what they most want to write about. Ask your students to make lists of topics they would like to write about. They can make lists at later points in the writing process, too.

Webbing

A great strategy that many teachers use with their students in all subjects is webbing, or making semantic webs. The simplest web is one with a topic in the center and supporting details radiating out like spokes on a wheel. There are all kinds of graphic organizers that students can use to organize the material that they wish to write about. (See Worksheet 6 in the Appendix.) Some teachers have found the use of an audiotape to be successful with students who resist writing things down. Try it.

Drawing

Invite students to draw pictures about an event or feeling and then write about the drawing. This is a useful strategy for younger children, but it can be used by students of all ages, especially those who are visual learners who may have trouble getting involved in writing.

Talking

Most students are comfortable with swapping topic ideas with a peer, or with you or another adult. Sharing ideas is an effective way to help kids think out loud, clarify their ideas, and see if they have something workable to write about. Peers can be their most valuable editors, from the prewriting stage onward, provided you model for them how to give constructive criticism.

Writer's Notebook

Invite students to keep a Writer's Notebook in which they record topic ideas, descriptions, story ideas, and snippets of events they might use one day in a story. Encourage them to write in this notebook on a regular basis, even a few times each day. Much like a painter's sketchbook, this notebook is a tool many working writers use to support their craft; introducing it in your classroom will help your students think of themselves as serious writers.

Writing Strategies

Review a Specific Writing Skill in Each Session

At the beginning of each writing session, give a short demonstration that helps your students use a certain writing skill. Try to keep the lesson under ten minutes. The purpose of the writing session is to write.

Set Aside Uninterrupted Time for Writing

Many teachers have found that reserving the first ten to fifteen minutes of the writing time for whole-class,

Third-graders brainstorm an A–Z list of possible writing topics.

uninterrupted writing works well. After that, children can continue to write while you hold conferences with individual students. Ideally, children should have writing time four or five days a week.

Rewriting Strategies

I do not think of rewriting as the copying of a draft onto clean paper or the typing of a piece on a keyboard to get it printed out. Rewriting is making changes in a draft, even if those changes are minor ones. Here is a short preview of rewriting strategies to use with your class:

Encourage Students to Reread Their Work

All writers should do this to get a sense of the piece as it develops. Demonstrate for kids how you might reread a piece as you write and after you have finished a draft.

Help Kids Understand Why They Are Revising

Find ways to show children why revision is so important. You might show students a first and final draft of a letter you wrote to a relative or to the local paper or samples of first and final drafts from former students. Children need to see with their own eyes that revision makes writing clearer—and more interesting to read.

Set Up Conference Routines

Invite students to choose a conference partner to whom they will read aloud their work. Remind them to pay close attention to their partner's work and comments. (For more on conferences, see Chapter 3, "Start With the Conference.") The conference should give students ideas of what to add or change. Hold class discussions that help kids learn to walk the fine line between using peers' suggestions and remaining true to their vision of the piece.

Set Up Editing Steps

After students are satisfied with their final drafts and have chosen to publish their pieces, it is time for editing. (See Chapter 8, "When and How to Polish and Edit.") They should first make their own editing corrections and then submit their piece to a peer editor. Only after all of this occurs do you, the teacher, do the final editing.

Invite Your Students to Publish the Finished Piece

There are various ways that a piece is prepared for publishing. Today many students type the piece on the computer and then print it out. They are also encouraged to rewrite the finished piece on clean paper. Some students then add a cover to the piece or make a book out of it by binding it in some way. These published pieces may be displayed in the classroom or school library. The piece may be included in a literary publication or a class newsletter. Students may read aloud their published pieces to their parents at a writers' tea or to younger students in their classrooms.

The Teacher as Writer

Doing the writing process with children requires a great deal of dedication on the part of the teacher. These days we are very aware of the importance of our students seeing with their own eyes what must be done, not simply being told what to do by the teacher at the front of the room. Showing children models of what to do helps them to be successful. You, the teacher, become the model of what a writer is supposed to do and to be. You need to convey to your students your own love of words, books, and writing. This is essential. Whether or not you yourself are an active writer is not as important as your attitude toward writing. Of course any writing you do, even if it is only a little sample of writing to share with your students, is a very special contribution to the effectiveness of your writing program.

Children have strong positive reactions to hearing the teacher's own stories. The more you write with children, the more their writing—and their attitude toward writing—will improve.

Don't underestimate the amount of work that goes into the use of the writing process. The writing sessions are completely individualized; your students are all writing on different topics, at their own pace and level of ability, and are making their own decisions about what to revise and how to revise it. None of this is easy for either the student or the teacher. Problems and questions arise constantly. There are no simple and certain answers because the effective teaching of writing is a complex process, and getting students to write effectively is even more complex. However, your dedication to the process can help your students produce startlingly original writing of high quality. The results can be thrilling.

CHAPTER 2

Create a Supportive Environment

Within the classroom itself building a supportive context for working collaboratively and sharing writing is perhaps the most important step a teacher can take to promote writing growth.

—Steven Zemelman, Harvey Daniels, Arthur Hyde, *Best Practices*

How to Create the Right Climate

Because of the understandable emotional overtones of the revision task, it is very important for you to create a climate that is emotionally safe for your students. This goes far beyond the writing lesson. It reaches into all of the personal and task-oriented interactions of the classroom.

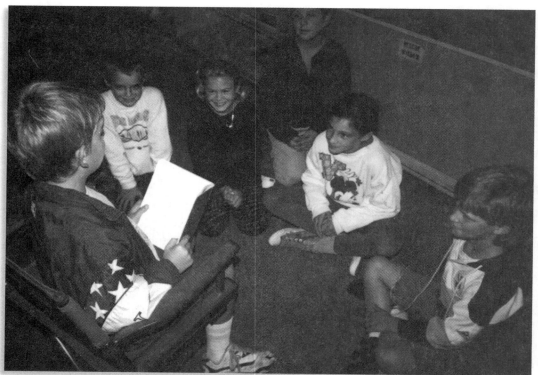

Third-grader Ross reads his amusing writing-journal piece to his peers. Modeling good listening skills pays off in more productive writing shares.

Students in grades two through six are at various stages of comfort with peers and with their teachers. Some children beg to be the center of attention; others simply sink back into themselves if they are chosen to stand out from the group in any way. We need to be aware of this; what is emotionally satisfying for one child might be humiliating for another. Know your students. Know who their friends are and who they are most comfortable with. Those are not necessarily the same people. Sometimes it's a good idea to simply ask them—in private, of course.

Writing itself is a private activity, even though the audience or reader of the piece is an integral part of the process of deciding what, how, and for whom one should write. If the audience is left out, the drive and focus of the piece will be missing. Of course, the audience may be oneself, but even then, if there is any intention to share the piece with someone, that future reader must be taken into account.

Self-consciousness arises from the fear of what that unknown reader will think of our writing efforts. This is perfectly natural. Adult writers have these same fears. The best way to confront these fears is to hang the writing out for all to see, or for at least one person to see. This is where the writers' workshop comes in. It is mainly a community of writers supporting one another to produce the best pieces of writing each is capable of. Teachers and students do that by sharing the writing with one another and by giving one another feedback. This sharing will only work if they listen to, respect, and support one another. You can do much to ensure that that happens.

How do we create a supportive community of writers? Here are some practical things we can do:

Observe and address classroom interactions.

Watch your students, especially when they work in groups. Ask yourself what is going on and why. Then ask some of the children. They usually know better than you, although they are sometimes hesitant to say. For example, there might be a child who is making fun of others. The children might be afraid that if they call attention to it, it might happen to them, too. It will take some gentle conversations and reassurances on your part to help that child to relax enough to share his or her worries with you.

Build listening skills.

You are the best model for your students. Look at the child who is speaking. Nod your head to show that you are listening. Focus the attention of the group on the speaker. Try not to repeat any of your questions or directions; to do so sends the message that one does not have to listen the first time around. Respond to what a child says by referring to aspects of it in your response, thereby showing that you really listened.

Give deliberate messages that promote an atmosphere of respect and trust.

Here are some messages that you may wish to write on a wall chart in your classroom:

* Listen to others as you would like others to listen to you.

* Find the particular thing that you liked in someone's writing and make a positive comment about it.

* Ask a question about something you didn't understand or something you are curious about.

* Share some suggestions you might have with your fellow writers, but remember that they must choose what to do with their pieces.

Help your students to develop a good attitude toward writing.

Your students have to develop an attitude toward writing that is positive and exciting. They need to know what writing is. Brainstorm with your students a chart of their ideas about what writing is and what it isn't. On the following page is an example of what they might share.

WHAT WRITING IS NOT:	WHAT WRITING IS:
❀ Something that you just have to get done and forget.	❀ A chance to tell about something clearly.
❀ An assignment that the teacher gives you.	❀ Thoughts on paper that sometimes come out quickly and easily, but usually take quite a bit of thought and rewriting.
❀ The same as talking.	❀ Words used to make sense to the reader and to stir up the reader's interest.
	❀ A way to find out what you already know.
	❀ A way to learn about yourself—what you think and feel.

The key idea to get across to students is that writing doesn't flow from the pen as polished prose. Children need to know that writing is a process—that they can improve a piece of writing by adding words, by removing words, and by changing words. Children in grades two through six need to know what writing is and how it differs from speaking. You can help them understand this by discussing such questions as: Are saying something and writing something the same thing? How are they the same? How are they different? Developing a class chart like the one shown at left can help kids keep in mind the differences between spoken and written language.

Emphasize to children that people write for real purposes, whether they write something as simple as a shopping list or as complex as a mystery. When students write with purpose, it's thrilling. For example, when I stepped into the school nurse's office one morning, third-grader Danny was showing her the baby bird that he just found outside. I was somewhat alarmed that the bird would not survive without its mother.

HOW WRITING DIFFERS FROM SPEAKING

Speaking comes out the way it is and it is gone (unless someone has recorded the words or even copied whatever is said word-for-word on paper).

Writing is different. Writing consists of putting words on paper. The words remain the same, or are changed if the writer wants to change them. In any case, the writer looks at the writing and makes a decision. The writer asks herself or himself: Have I said what I meant to say?

Riva Fisher, our nurse, encouraged Danny to go out and look for the mother bird. He did, and then he gave me the news about what happened by writing me this letter. It's a great example of real-life writing:

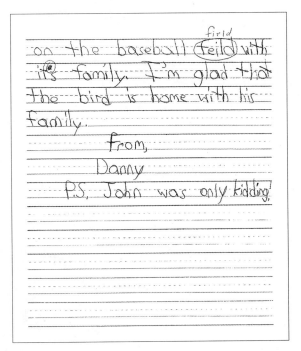

> Dear Dr. Tully
> The bird that I found is all right. He got back to his family. The bird was so cute. It's colors were white, yellow, brown, and black. The way I caught it's because of John and Billy. John told Jeremy to step on it, but I told Jeremy not to. After, Mrs. Davidson and I went out and put the bird on the baseball feild [field] with it's family. I'm glad that the bird is home with his family.
> From,
> Danny
> P.S. John was only kidding!

Children also need to be reassurred that writing happens at different paces, depending on all sorts of factors. At times they will have a full story right in their heads and can quickly tell the story aloud or write the story on paper. At other times, they may have a simple idea, image or feeling that interests them. They might write these impressions or ideas in a notebook and let them germinate for a few days before trying to develop them into a story. They may spend hours writing only to find out there isn't a story after all, or they may spend hours and wind up with a jewel of a story. Let children know that professional writers experience these ebbs and flows of creativity all the time.

Encourage children to celebrate the process of writing by letting them know that:

- ☀ they can experiment, using trial and error.

- ☀ they can think and figure things out.

- ☀ they can see with their own eyes that they can make a story better.

- ☀ they can decide to change something or not.

- ☀ practice makes it easier.

Plan Classroom Space

Before you launch your writing program, give some thought to the layout of the classroom. Aim to provide classroom spaces that allow for uninterrupted writing. Over the course of the week, two-thirds of the total writing time should be spent actually writing; conferences and mini-lessons on writing skills and strategies take up the remaining time. On certain days, you will want to devote the entire session to writing; at other times, conferences will take precedence. With this in mind, how can you design the room to reflect your writers' workshop?

Many teachers have children write at their regular desks and invite children to a conference area for peer and teacher-student conferences. They set up these areas around a table, on the outskirts of the room, or on the rug areas. For younger students, a rug makes a great gathering place. Middle- and upper-elementary students may enjoying reading their piece aloud to their peers from a lectern set up in the conference area. For one-on-one conferences, some teachers prefer to improvise, using floor space by the clothing closets, hallways, or other quiet spots.

Writing areas may be marked with signs on a bulletin board or by displaying signs that you can make like this:

Hallways make great quiet writing areas.

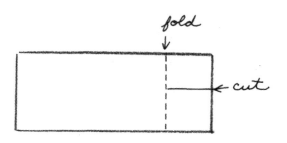

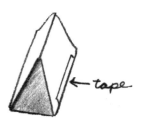

fold in thirds and tape edges together

← tape

Prepare Writers' Materials

*W*riting materials are simple and straightforward. Pencil and paper is all a writer really needs. However, there are some writers' tools that can be helpful to have on hand:

- Off-white, yellow, or other neutral-color lined paper for writing drafts is a good basic; for the final copy, white lined paper is ideal. Printing the piece on a computer gives a polished look, but hand-written final copy captures a child's personality in ways that a computer can't. Such handwritten samples can be a treasure for you, for parents, and even for the children themselves in later years.

Third-grader Julia inputs her edits on a computer.

- A computer with a word processing program can be highly motivating in that it allows students to revise and edit without having to rewrite every draft from scratch. Children love computer graphics, and scanning in their illustrations or photographs can be powerful additions to a published piece.

- Colored pencils and thin-tipped markers are great for making editing marks because they are easy to see. (See Chart 8 in the Appendix for a list of editing marks to share with kids.) Use highlighting markers to flag sentences that belong together in the same paragraph.

- Date stamps are popular with children for marking drafts and documenting what was written and when. A stamp with the words "Draft" or "Only a Draft—Spelling Doesn't Yet Count" or "Work in Progress" is useful for helping parents understand, when work goes home, that you are not looking for perfect spelling, etc., during the early drafts of writing.

- Scissors and tape for cutting and pasting (unless one is cutting and pasting on the computer) help kids visualize and reorganize their pieces.

- Stick-on notes are great flags on which you and students can write revision notes, questions, and so forth.

- Pressure-sensitive dots and other color labels can help kids organize their revision plans. For example, green dots can designate places in the text that need more detail, yellow dots can signal where to add dialogue, and so on.

- Colorful paper clips are good for marking paragraphs that need more work; kids can use them to clip sections that need to be added to or deleted from the text.

Sixth-grade writers at work.

Stick to Routines

*I*t is important for students to be able to count on writing sessions at set times each week. Large blocks of time work best. For younger students, try to schedule at least an hour per session. Middle school schedules usually allow only 40–50 minutes, but with good time management, this time can be very productive. Devoting sufficient time to a writing workshop is crucial, as it allows the full writing cycle to be played out and accommodates the learning styles of children who take a while to get on task.

Give students the opportunity to write every day. This is not always possible, I know, given the demands of the curriculum. Three times a week is the absolute minimum; writing fewer times keeps children from gaining momentum. It is always good practice to end a session with a lot of excitement about what's to follow. With that motivation urging them on, it's a shame not to build on it in the next day or two while it's still fresh.

If you can manage it, the first hour each morning is excellent for writing. The most important thing is to make writing a priority. Don't squeeze it into that odd twenty minutes between gym and lunch. Some teachers have had success with the first hour after lunch every day because the social interactions at lunchtime or recess seem to prime kids for writing about personal experiences. The writing also has the power to calm children down after active play.

The writing session itself can be divided into the following slots of time:

5–10 minutes	Group Work: Mini-Lesson on a Selected Topic
30–40 minutes	Individual Writing and Peer or Teacher Conferences
5–10 minutes	Group Work: Sharing the Writing

CHAPTER 3

Start with the Conference

An essential element for good writing is a good ear: One must listen to the sound of one's own prose.
—Barbara Tuchman, in *The Writer's Art*

Key Ideas

*W*riting conferences are an integral part of revision. Writing moves forward faster when it is shared with others who can help clarify topic, tone, audience, characters, and so on. A classmate's enthusiastic response to a story or a chuckle from you at a line of dialogue spur a child on. Before discussing conferences in more detail, here are a few key ideas I'd like to share about your role in children's writing process.

Do all that you can do to support the efforts of the children as writers.

If you get a sense that helping them to pick topics that have a strong hold on them will be beneficial, spend a lot of time on generating topics. If you find that they shut down when you require them to do an outline before writing, don't do it. What works for some will not work for others. Allow for a spontaneous, creative piece to flow from the pen without the requirement of using every step of the process. Varied purposes and genres will have varied approaches.

Give children ownership of their work as writers.

It has got to be theirs. For the writing bug to bite, they've got to be excited about the power they have to express their thoughts and to tell their own stories. They have to choose their own topics and to revise as they are aware and able. It is important to guide them to look squarely at their own pieces and to reflect on them.

Have high expectations of excellence and hard work.

Don't let students settle for a weak piece of writing. Let them know that writing is not easy and that you will be giving them tools to help them. Guide students to be able to handle the difficulties by building their writing and revision skills as they work. For example, show them revision techniques such as reading a piece aloud to oneself to listen for clunky dialogue, descriptions that are too vague, and so forth. They need to learn what makes a good piece of writing and how they can make their first drafts into good pieces of writing. Communicate to them the importance of what they are doing.

> *The conference is where the writer first shares the piece with an outside audience.*

The Writing Conference

*T*he most important tool for revision is the conference. This is where the writer first shares the piece with an audience outside himself and sees his work from a greater distance. Writing is communication, and the conference brings this reality home to the young writer in a very real way. The conference can offer the writer a wonderful opportunity to have the one-on-one attention of an adult (in most cases the teacher, although it could be a parent, principal, or adult volunteer; it could also be a fellow student). Conferences take many forms. On the next page is an overview of the various types of conferences that a student might have.

Fifth graders peer-edit each other's work.

ONE-TO-ONE CONFERENCES:

- ✹ Student-to-teacher

- ✹ Student-to-student

These are the most common, but here are some innovative pairings:

- ✹ Student-to-older student

- ✹ Student-to-principal

- ✹ Student-to-parent or grandparent

- ✹ Student-to-volunteer adult (This could be a senior volunteer.)

ONE-TO-GROUP CONFERENCES:

- ✹ Sharing with the whole class or with a smaller group

- ✹ Writers' Circle: Each member of the group takes a turn sharing the piece with the others.

The most common type of group conference is one in which a student reads the piece aloud to the whole class and then students respond with questions and comments. The conference is especially effective when a writer asks for specific help. For example, a student might say, "I'm having trouble trying to figure out an exciting first sentence. Any ideas?"

I have found that once you and your students build a feeling of community, students are sensitive, perceptive, and direct with one another about their work.

How to Conduct a Writers' Conference With Students

Here are some steps to share with anyone who is conferring with a young writer. I developed them to help volunteers know how to guide a conference. (See Chart 3 in the Appendix for a quick check you can post in your classroom or distribute.)

Listen carefully as the child reads the piece aloud to you.

Even if the child struggles to read aloud, or if it takes a long time, don't skip or shortcut this step. Reading aloud allows the child to hear the piece, its language and rhythms, and to catch things that are missing or need to be

changed. It also reinforces the idea that writing is always for an audience. The child's tone and emotional reaction as he or she reads or talks about the piece can give you valuable insight into the real story—that is, the story that is hinted at but not yet told in this draft.

Third-grade teacher Donna Schaefer confers with Clarisa about her story beginning.

Comment briefly about your reaction to the piece.

The writer needs an immediate audience reaction such as "Thanks for reading your story to me. I like how you write," or "That was quite a story." The writer needs to know that his or her work counts.

Ask questions.

"How do you feel about your story so far?" is a good question to start the conference. Then, you might simply ask the writer to explain a part that was not clear, or ask, "Can you tell me more about . . . ?" Through your questions, try to help the writer to figure out the part of the story that really grabs his or her interest. In the next draft, this will become the heart of the piece. You're always helping the child move toward the heart of it all—the truthful, powerful emotion hidden between the lines of brief, even bland first drafts.

Help the writer to discover for himself or herself what needs to be changed in the story.

You cannot tell the writer what to do. The writer must be in charge of his or her own writing. That's what being an author means—being the creator or originator, that is, the author-ity. A writer often does not want to make any changes in the piece. That must be respected. You might encourage the writer to ask you for whatever help he or she might want.

Before closing this conference, ask the writer what he or she plans to do with the piece.

This reminds students of what, specifically, to focus on when they return to their desks to revise. A child might reply, "I want to go back and add that part about my dog that I told you about." You can give some reminders of your conversation, but do not tell the child what to add or change. You might like to close with a comment about the process—for example, "I am curious to see how your piece develops as you work on it. I look forward to reading the story again."

Questions to Ask During a Conference

The questions that follow—which are not in any particular order—can help guide you as you hold conferences with students. (See Chart 4 in the Appendix for a poster version of this.)

QUESTIONS FOR WRITERS—TRY SOME!

1. How do you feel about your story so far?

2. Are you finished, or do you want to write more? What are you planning to write?

3. What part works the best for you? Why?

4. What part, if any, does not work for you? Do you want to get rid of it, or do you want to change it?

5. Tell me more about . . . .

6. Is there anything unusual about . . . ?

7. I don't understand what you meant when you wrote . . . .

8. Why did you choose this topic?

9. Did you say what you really wanted to in this piece?

10. Who are you writing this for? (Who is your audience?)

11. What is your purpose in writing this piece?

12. What title would you give this piece?

CHAPTER 4

Teach How to Revise

Then rising with Aurora's light,
The muse invoked, sit down to write,
Blot out, correct, insert, refine,
Enlarge, diminish, interline.

—Jonathan Swift, "On Poetry," 1733

In the previous chapter I shared strategies for getting children to think about their writing and share it with their classmates in a one-on-one or group conference or with you. Now comes the hard part—getting them to go back and actually revise their writing. But it can be done!

First, students need to know what to shoot for, what the target is. They need to know what an unrevised piece and a revised piece look like and why one is better than the other. Once they can evaluate drafts and recognize the difference between rough copy and finely honed prose, they need to know how to apply this knowledge to their own work. And they need to be motivated to do it. Another way of saying all this is that you need to teach them how to revise.

Very few of your students will be able to do this intuitively. Here are the steps you need to take:

1. **Model what revision looks like.**

2. **Show and evaluate the difference between drafts.**

3. **Help students apply revision skills to their own writing.**

4. **Practice revision.**

5. **Build motivation.**

This is a tall order. Students need to use the higher-level thinking skill of evaluation, and that's always a challenge. And it involves the more difficult and essential job of getting your students to *want* to revise.

Looking at the list above, you might have noticed that these steps are the same ones that every good teacher uses to help children learn any skill. These are the steps that a person who doesn't know how to do something can follow to learn to do it well. By looking at the model and practicing, the apprentice can become an expert.

> *If our kids are going to become expert writers, they must become expert revisers.*

STEP 1:
Model What Revision Looks Like

There are many ways to model the revision process for students. In fact, you can create different ways as you proceed. The following chapter will provide many examples of ways to model revision. Here we'll look at one idea that may be the most effective starting point you can use.

Demonstrate the process by revising in front of your students. That is, think of an incident in your life or a description and jot it down on chart paper or the board. Keep it brief, so it's easy to work with, and deliberately make it plain. See the model below.

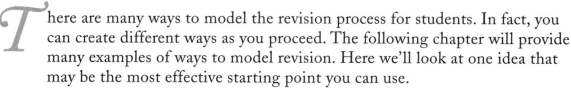

My friend has a cat. The cat is tan and black. She likes to climb. She is funny and smart.

Ask students to comment on the draft. They might like it, but try to show them that it really isn't very interesting; it doesn't grab the interest of the reader.

Invite them to ask you questions to fill out the incident or description.

Suggest that they ask: "How did you feel when . . . ?" "Is there anything unusual about . . . ?"

Accept all of their questions and comments, but lead them to ask the questions that will get you to rehearse the real story with them. (See Draft 2 for the real story.) Then ask for volunteers to raise their hands and give suggestions. The whole class will thus help you to write the second draft on the board. Here are some types of questions you might like to ask:

❀ Who can give me a first sentence that immediately grabs the interest of the reader?

❀ What should we write next?

❀ What about setting the scene?

❀ Who can give me a good ending?

Second-grader Amanda writes a first sentence on the chart.

For each of these questions, I would accept possibilities from two or more students and then choose the one that says it best. That alone is modeling the revision process; every writer thinks of various possibilities and then chooses the one that works the best.

Take a look at Draft 2. It is the result of what a third-grade class came up with when they attacked my boring first draft—not bad for eight- and nine-year-olds! You may want to show your students this draft after sharing and discussing the first draft. You may also share it with them after they try writing their own second draft of the piece. They then can compare the two second drafts and discuss which is better and why. Or, you may simply want them to look at my first and second drafts and compare them. After that, you may want to try it with a little story of yours or a story by one of your students. Remember, the first one should be dull on purpose, with the real story being more dynamic.

DRAFT #1

My friend has a cat. The cat is tan and black. She likes to climb. She is funny and smart.

DRAFT #2

The Baseball Cat

My friend Anna has an amazing and unusual cat named Kika. This cat goes into the kitchen and she climbs up and stands on the edge of the sink. First she stares at the end of the faucet. The drop of water gets bigger and bigger. Suddenly the drop starts to fall. Kika swings her paw fast and she hits the drop and makes a grand slam!

STEP 2:
Show and Evaluate the Difference Between Drafts

*W*e have already begun to look at the difference between a revised and an unrevised piece. This step involves looking at pieces more deliberately and analyzing the difference. This step can also use the ideas and models from the chapter that follows.

Students must grasp the concept that revision makes a piece better.

For students to be able to revise, they must grasp the concept that revision is a way of making a piece of writing better—that is, closer to what you want to communicate to the reader and a clearer, more engaging piece of writing for the reader to read.

Show students a sample of a first draft and a completed second draft of the same piece. The drafts could be duplicated and distributed to each child, or they could be put on a transparency and projected onto a screen or wall with an overhead projector. The important thing is that the whole class, or a small group, is working on analyzing the piece together.

Here's an example of two drafts that a second-grade class examined, and the reasons they discovered for why the second draft worked better than the first.

Here is a little story that I wrote about my niece's dog. I pretended that I was she, and that the dog was my dog:

DRAFT #1

I love my dog. He is so cute and fluffy. I play with him. His name is Corky.

DRAFT #2

Here's how I changed, or revised, that little story:

A Friend Who Loves Books

I have a friend who is always there, always ready to play, always nice to me. His name is Corky. He is a little dog with curly black fur.

I love my Corky. He is so cute and fluffy. I play with him. He licks my face and then I have to wash it off. He makes me laugh.

He is a very smart dog who enjoys books. When my dad is ready to read to me, Corky scrambles up on my bed, snuggles in, and listens to every word. He is an amazing dog.

Read aloud the first and second drafts. Ask your students what the difference is between the two pieces. Try to elicit responses like these:

the second one has a title

it is longer

it is more interesting

it made me see the dog in my mind

it's funnier

it reminded me of my dog

it tells what the dog does

it's more real

it gives more details

Write a summary of the discussion on the chalkboard, or have students develop their observations into a chart to which they can add ideas as the lessons progress. At right is a sample chart.

REASONS WHY THE SECOND DRAFT WORKED BETTER:

1. *It is a topic you care about.*

2. *The writing is more interesting.*

3. *The piece has a lot of detail.*

4. *It has more feeling.*

The children came up with the list quite readily, in part because their teacher had worked with them on the qualities of good writing in earlier mini-lessons.

While children need to learn how to evaluate the improvement between a first and second draft, they also should know that there are times when the first draft is a better piece of writing than the second. Revision isn't a linear path to improvement—sometimes later drafts don't have the spark of the first writing.

STEP 3:
Help Students Apply Revision Skills to Their Own Writing

Okay, so how do we get students into the swing of revising their own pieces? For a start, use the technique that I described above and ask students to try it out for themselves. Invite them to think of a little incident or story that has a twist, or something unusual about it. Then they should deliberately try to write a dull first draft. Make it short and make sure that there is no action. Then ask them to try to write the exciting or unusual story.

Let them know that this is merely an exercise or a

> *Some kinds of spontaneous writing truly don't need a second draft at all. It often depends on the nature of the writing.*

Sixth-grader Adeoluwa reflects on his story revision.

34

game. You know that they would usually try to write the best they could first time around.

Through these practices, kids gain firsthand experience in noting the difference between the first and second drafts. Because you're inviting them to write in two different ways on purpose, they do not have to feel that they did something less than perfect for the first draft—that's precisely what they set out to do!

STEP 4:
Practice Revision

*T*he next step is for your class to get right down to the task of revising their own pieces. This can take place right after they have had a chance to write their first draft even if it's just the first paragraph or two. They should keep the piece of writing short. Children get very discouraged when they have to revise long pieces. Remember, they are in the stage of learning to revise, and learning works best if the focus is clear and simple.

Limit the first revision lessons to short pieces.

There are always a few students who finish their pieces in a very short time. Let them be the models for the others. This is a good opportunity to have a mini-lesson in the middle of the writing session rather than at the beginning, because then you will be able to use a freshly written piece for a model.

Invite a child to read his or her piece of writing to the class. Here's an example of one such piece.

DRAFT #1:

by Stephanie, grade 3

I have a hamster named Jumper. He likes to jump. When I first got him, he jumped in the cage so much that he hit his head on his water bottle.

Use this piece to apply one suggestion for revision. Then suggest that the whole class try to use that same suggestion on their pieces. The suggestion might be the following: Begin your piece with a lively sentence or two that really grabs the interest of the reader.

Here is how Stephanie chose to begin her second draft. In her final draft, Stephanie added more details, and ended her story with as much verve as she opened it.

DRAFT #2:

The Jumping Hamster

by Stephanie, Grade 3

"Ow! I think I need a doctor. I might have a concussion. I need a phone to make an appointment. Help me out of this cage!" said my hamster to himself.

My funny hamster is named Jumper. He likes to jump so much that he jumps all day. When I first got him, he kept jumping up and down so high that he hit the top of his head on his water bottle.

FINAL DRAFT:

The Jumping Hamster

by Stephanie, Grade 3

"Ow! I think I need a doctor. I might have a concussion. I need a phone to make an appointment. Help me out of this cage!" said my hamster to himself.

My funny hamster is named Jumper. He likes to jump so much that he jumps all day. When I first got him, he kept jumping up and down so high that he hit the top of his head on his water bottle.

One day after I went to give him food, I saw something even worse. He had gotten two of his teeth stuck into the top screen of the cage. He was struggling to get out. My cat Josh was standing by the cage hissing at him. So I screamed, "Mon, get Josh out of here. The hamster's in big trouble. Josh is driving him crazy."

So my mom held the hamster and lifted the screen up at the same time and got the teeth free.

"Thank God I'm free!" said Jumper.

Here are some of the ways in which a writer can start a piece so that it creates interest immediately. (See Chart 6 in the Appendix.)

- ☼ Use a lively quotation.

- ☼ Use dialogue.

- ☼ Say something unusual.

- ☼ Create a sense of drama.

- ☼ Mention a strange or interesting place.

- ☼ Use action words.

- ☼ Use exclamations.

- ☼ Use humor.

- ☼ Present a problem.

> **Make a table or bulletin board display of students' story beginnings. Display selections of great beginnings from published books alongside your students' own writings.**

Invite the whole class to revise their pieces immediately (even if they are not finished with their first draft), adding a new beginning that gets the reader to pay attention. They may wish to refer to the above list for ideas. Make sure that children know why the new beginning is better than their original beginning. Their previous work on revision should give them the basis for seeing and judging the difference.

Give them a set amount of time to do this. At the end of that time, ask students to pick partners and share their old and new openings with each other. If anyone is stuck, they can offer each other suggestions. Ask for a few volunteers to share their beginnings with the whole class.

Now talk with students about looking at their piece with an eye to infusing it with more emotion. Can they add words that convey feeling? Can they name for themselves the feeling one character has for another? Can they open the story with a situation in which that feeling is revealed?

Third graders learn that good beginning sentences hook the reader.

Jonathan wrote this as his first draft:

My Friend Lee

Lee is a kid in my class. He has blonde hair and is tall. Sometimes I play with his brother.

Then Jonathan added feelings and came up with this:

My friend Lee is close to me. I like him and he likes me. We are best friends. Sometimes I play with his brother. We are best friends too. How is your friend? We once built a fort. We have a password that I cannot tell you.

You can see how Jonathan added how he felt about his friend. He also added details that are very special to him. There is a lot of feeling in this little piece. Sometimes children find a powerful voice when they choose a new topic. Third-grader Nick told me that he was bored with writing all of the time about his baseball games. I asked, "Why not write about a trip?" So, he wrote about Hawaii, a place that he had visited when he was about six.

Surfers

By Nick

Dedicated to George, Evelyn, Chris, and Johnny

Two summers ago, I went to the coolest place in the world, Hawaii. When I was there, I saw about thirteen surfers. I wanted to know how to surf, so I asked my dad if I could get a surfboard. I thought he'd say yes, but he said no.

I tried surfing without a surfboard and I fell under the wave. My brother saved me, but after that he beat me up. My brother also said that there was a shark in the water.

"I'm swimming, I'm swimming!"

I was so happy, I was waving my arms around like I was a hero. By accident I hit my brother in the stomach.

A week after that we went home. I didn't learn how to surf, but at least I learned how to swim!

There are an unlimited number of strategies that writers can use to improve their writing. These can be introduced to your students one at a time as they practice their revisions; students respond better in the beginning if you limit their choices. In Chapter 6—"A Selection of Mini-Lessons for Revision," I include a mini-lesson on each of seven revision strategies. In the meantime, students may wish to review their writing alone or with a conference partner. Perhaps these questions can help them get started. (See Chart 7 in the Appendix.)

ASK THESE QUESTIONS TO IMPROVE YOUR WRITING:

1. *What title do I want?*

2. *Does my first sentence make people want to read more?*

3. *Is the piece about one main idea? (Is it focused?)*

4. *Does the writing say what I want it to say?*

5. *Who is going to read this? (Who is my audience?)*

6. *Does it make sense?*

7. *Does this piece fulfill the purpose I had in writing it?*

8. *Did I end it well?*

Add to this chart as your students discover more revision prompts of their own.

STEP 5:
Build Motivation

Students need to hear and see revision at work throughout the school year. They need to have plenty of practice in recognizing and appreciating the difference between revised and unrevised pieces of their own and of peers. They've got to see it with their own eyes and hear it with their own ears. They

> *Students need to buy into revision because revision is hard work.*

have to bask in the benefits of revision, whether that be a rousing round of applause from their peers when they read aloud their final draft, or a peer calling out, "Great story!" in the hallway, or an expression on your face that lets them know they've written something that moved you.

Unless we motivate children by teaching them the tools of writing and showing them how their writing matters to others, they will not sustain the effort of revising. In time, the motivation to write well will come from within each child. For now, we must guide our students toward that state of inner motivation. One of the most powerful ways you can do this is to help children choose topics that they care about. Here are some suggestions for creating opportunities for children to get caught up in their writing:

Make writing fun.

Make the writing session into a type of game-playing, so that children feel comfortable trying things out, pushing the rules, using trial and error, attempting various strategies, competing against their own sense of what they want to accomplish, and surpassing their own early efforts (second draft surpasses their first draft).

Take a look at the piece below—it's a good example of how students can inject fun into revising and publishing. Anella's teacher told me that "Queen Gussy" grew out of a medieval-theme unit. Anella wrote the story and then made some changes and additions to it. When she shared it with her friends, they liked it so much they turned it into a little skit and performed it for the whole class.

Queen Gussy

By Anella

In the little town of Kramer there lived a poor young maiden who worked for the queen. The maiden had no name and the queen would call her Dustball, for that is what she looked like. All day she was cleaning and dusting, and at night she slept in the attic which was filled with dust.

One day as the maiden was getting ready to clean she heard a little voice call out"Boy is this place dusty. Achoo!" The maiden turned around and to her surprise found a little gray mouse wearing a green and black checkered t-shirt and pink shoes.

"Who are you?" asked the maiden.

"Are you talking to me?" asked the little mouse.

"Well sure I am!"

"I have been living in this dust yard for two months already, and it's about time you cleaned this place up, "said the mouse in his loudest voice, which was very quiet to the maiden. By the way, my name is Gussy.

"I was going to do that tonight. It's just that I've been cleaning this whole house, and I just don't have the time. The queen never gives me a break."

"Well I think I have an idea" said Gussy. "How would you like to be queen?"

"How in the world is that going to happen?"

The mouse motioned for the maiden to come down to his mouth and then whispered a brilliant idea.

The next week the young maiden had become queen and her name was Queen Gussy.

P.S.—No one knows what Gussy whispered to the maiden, but whatever he did, it worked.

Create a sense that they are part of a whole—a sense of belonging to the writers' group.

Your classroom becomes a writers' workshop where each child gives it his or her best shot and where each person supports the others.

Give children the freedom to develop as writers.

This means that they really must choose their own topics. You can, however, limit the choices. For example, it is perfectly fine to limit the writing to personal-experience writing or to limit the particular revision skill that is currently being practiced. But to build motivation, students must have choices of topic and expression. They must have choices about who they'd like to have as conference partners. They should even have choices about where in the room they can have the conference. They must have the freedom to revise as they see fit, unless it is simply an exercise that they are doing as they learn a revision skill. Below and on page 42 is a great example of revision at work. The early draft was rambling and has plenty of changes. This piece conveys David's enthusiasm for this wonderful dog.

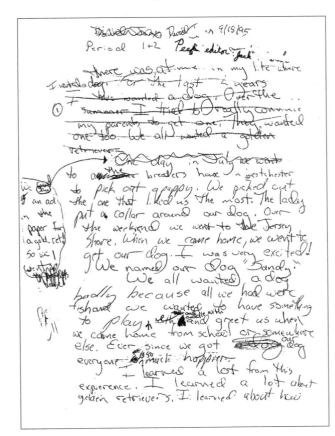
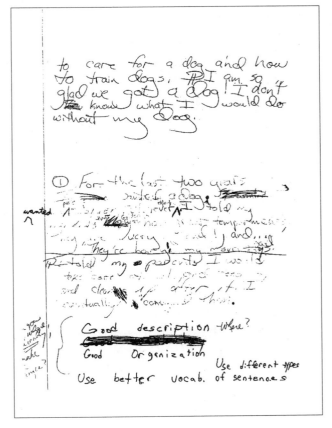

> ## What I Wanted the Most
>
> ### By David
>
> For the last two years I have wanted a dog. I wanted a pure bread golden retriever to be exact. I told my parents that golden retrievers have great temperaments, they are very friendly and... "They are hair," my mom said. I told my parents I would take care of it, feed it, and clean up after it. I eventually convinced them with the help from my friend who has three dogs.
>
> We found an ad in the paper for a golden retriever! So we went to the breeders house in Westchester to pick out a puppy. We picked out the one that liked us the most. The lady put a collar around our dog. Over the weekend we went to the Jersey Shore. It was fun, but I wanted to get home to get my dog. When we came home, we went to get our dog. I was very excited! We named our dog "Sandy."
>
> We all wanted a dog badly because all we had were fish. We wanted to have something to play, and cuddle with and greet us when we got home from school or somewhere else. Ever since we got our dog, everyone is so much happier.
>
> I learned a lot from this experience. I learned many things about golden retrievers. I learned about how to care for a dog and how to train dogs. I got to like dogs much more than before. I absolutely love dogs now.
>
> I am so glad we got a dog! I don't know what I would do without my dog. He is very frisky, but he still is great. I think he is the greatest dog in the whole wide world.

Let them experience their power as writers.

This can be felt in the revision process as they improve their writing. The development of control enables them to avoid getting lost in a sense of helplessness or that anything goes. The greatest way to get a sense of their own power as writers is to see the effect of their writing on the reader. Give them opportunities to share their writing and opportunities to publish. The outside world will provide the greatest motivation of all to get it right. The outside world might only be the one person to whom your student is writing, but he or she surely wants to express effectively on paper what is on his or her mind. They can experience firsthand the difference in effect upon their readers of an unrevised and a revised piece. This can be a highly motivating experience in convincing them to work on their pieces.

These four motivators—fun, belonging, freedom, and power—are simple applications of some ideas from Adlerian psychology, as applied by William Glasser to schools (*Schools Without Failure*, NY: Harper, 1969). It is a useful schema to think about what motivates any of us to do anything. It can surely help us to motivate students to write and to learn.

Real-Life Motivators

Children are also motivated by meeting and finding out about real people in the world who write for a living or for pleasure. You, the teacher, are the most important model for this. Contact with authors, especially authors of the books that they are reading, is a powerful modeling experience for children. The contact might be in the form of a letter to the author or an authors' piece about how he or she writes. It always amazes children to hear that the famous author experiences the same types of problems that the child does. A classroom visit by an author is excellent, but it is rare because of the demands on most author's schedules. An audiotape or videotape of the author is a good stand-in.

It's important for teachers to motivate students by letting them know that revising is not just a school exercise. Many people use revision skills as part of their work.

JOBS THAT REQUIRE REVISION SKILLS:

Journalists revise stories.

The principal revises a letter to parents.

The manager revises a memo.

The pastor revises a sermon.

The high school senior revises the essay he has written in his college application.

Mom revises the note to the teacher about how the dog ate your homework.

Dad revises the shopping list.

The coach revises a letter of recommendation for you.

The police officer writes the report in full sentences from the notes.

The editor revises the book manuscript.

Models of Writing as Motivators

Nothing motivates students more than presenting them with actual models of revision. Give them plenty of examples. In the next chapter you will find ideas and models to use in your classroom. Clear and simple models will get children to think about possibilities for their own writing.

Summing Up

Revising is a skill, and, like any skill, it needs to be modeled, tried, practiced, and refined. It is hard work, and children need to be motivated to do it. As all good teachers do, you need to teach it and not expect that children can do it spontaneously. They need to be shown what to do. That's why models are so effective. "Show, don't tell," is a classic rule for good writing. Providing children with models is also an effective guideline for teaching in general.

CHAPTER 5

Compare Models of Revision

Writing begins with a leap of faith, with a decision to make meaning from a chosen thread, and the truth of the matter is that anything can start us on the road toward significance.

—Lucy McCormick Calkins, *The Art of Teaching Writing*

How to Use Models

In order to help children understand why it is worth their effort to think of better ways to write something, you need to provide plenty of models of revision to study and to work with. You might have already led them through the models you presented from Chapter 4, "Teach How to Revise," but that's only a beginning. You'll need to be constantly on the lookout for more models. By comparing these drafts with your students, you will help them to see the difference in the drafts before they can do it themselves.

When you want to share with a group of students the early and final drafts of a piece of writing, it works well to place both drafts on a transparency and use an overhead projector. Ask students to comment on the drafts, and try to direct the discussion toward the goal of understanding how the revisions have improved the writing. (There will always be students who try to get attention by saying that they like the first draft better. That's fine. Use it. It can lead to a great discussion about revision. And there is even a chance that the first draft *is* better!) Use the criteria of good writing to make the point. (See Worksheet 2 in the Appendix, "Portfolio Criteria.") Remember that short pieces are easier to use as models and can make the point more efficiently and more clearly.

> *Kids have to see the difference between the drafts.*

How to Find Models

Models can be found or created. The most direct way of finding a model as you are planning a lesson is to share your own students' writing with the class. You will find an unending supply of models from your students. Keep a file of early drafts and of final drafts of selected pieces. To get you started, I have placed a number of samples throughout the book. Feel free to use them, although the samples you find from your own students will surely be better. This is because you might be able to find a more dramatic difference between first and final drafts, and because the children always tune in to their own classmates. I caution you to do two things, however. First, make sure that you have each student's permission to share his or her piece, or, if they prefer, to present the piece without the author's name. Second, make sure that the piece is appropriate and illustrative of the focus of the lesson.

> *Direct the discussion toward the goal of understanding how the revisions have improved the writing.*

If you do any writing yourself, it is a great idea to share your drafts with your students. The first draft might be a description or image from your notebook. Then expand that into a short piece. This exercise might even help you with your own writing. Children love to critique adult writers.

You could do a quick piece of writing to use as you plan your lesson. It usually only takes a few minutes, whereas hunting for a sample from other sources can take hours. Feel free to use any of the samples from this book, of course, or collect samples of teachers' writing by asking your colleagues to share them with you. Grade-level differences are not important (with student samples as well).

Sixth-grader Diane reads aloud the story she has revised based on her peers' suggestions.

You may also find models of good writing from literature. Much research on works of famous authors is done by comparing early and late drafts of their writings. This gives scholars a chance to see the creative process at work. The problem is that most early drafts of literature that students are reading don't exist anymore, are not available to the general public, or the revisions are so subtle that the impact is lost on children.

Selections from literature can simply be presented as models of final drafts that are successful. Read directly from the published book that has the sample you have chosen. Here's an example from the opening of *Otis Spofford* by Beverly Cleary (Dell, 1953):

> There was nothing that Otis Spofford liked better than stirring up a little excitement. Otis was a medium-sized boy with reddish-brown hair, freckles, and ears that stuck out. He often wore a leather jacket with a rabbit's foot tied to the zipper, and he always laced his shoes with the kind of laces that glow in the dark—pink for the right shoe and green for the left.

This is what students can aim for. Students can also create some imaginary early drafts of these selections. See the section below for some ideas.

How to Create Models

As I suggested in Chapter 4, get your students into the game of writing drafts. Here are three approaches you might have fun using:

Fill in the Dots

Write a first and final draft yourself. On the next page is an example of a typical piece of writing that I have written and used with classes:

DRAFT #1

My Trip to My Grandmother's House

I got up early. We got ready. We drove about three hours. Grandma was happy to see us. We sat around and talked. We came home when it was dark and I went to bed.

Kids can write many of these bed-to-bed stories and they are all pretty much the same unless they "fill in the dots," writing about the particular, adding the contours and shadings of characters and events. That's the key—make it so particular that it can only be one child who has had that experience. Only then will it truly speak to our hearts.

Now let's look at "My Trip to My Grandmother's House." Rather, let's look at this experience, this little piece of life lived.

The interesting relationship is that between Grandma and the child. What happened? What was she doing? What is it that is strange or unusual about grandma?

I remember something unusual about my own grandma when I was eight or nine. Before the age of washing machines, she used to boil the kitchen towels in a big pot to get them clean. I remember how odd I found that to be. So I took that detail and expanded it for the second draft. The second draft is about an aspect I hardly mentioned in the first draft.

DRAFT #2

Towel Soup

Grandma's kitchen was warm and steamy. I saw that she was cooking something on the stove.

"Something smells good, Grandma," I said. "What's in the big pot?"

"My kitchen towels and dish rags," she answered.

"What? Towel soup? Yuk!" I said.

Grandma chuckled, "Silly. That's not for lunch." She saw my puzzled look. "I'm just boiling my towels. It loosens the dirt in them."

Use this piece as an example of how much more interesting a story can be when it involves a quirk or something unusual about a person, rather than yet another trip to see the person.

Bounce Back

Another way to work is to compare a final story with its early stages. Present the final version and study it. Then show the early version if you have it, or create one if you don't. Try doing that with a final copy of one of your student's pieces. Ask students to try to reconstruct what the first draft might have been like.

Reviser at work: Fifth-grader Danielle works on her story with her teacher, Eileen Miranda.

Here's a sample of a published piece from a third grader whom I taught about ten years ago. I no longer have his early drafts, but I did have this sample in my file:

There's a Mouse in the House

I was racing into the kitchen to get my candy. I was about to reach into the bag. There was something moving in the bag. I was beginning to be suspicious.

"I hope it's not a . . . Ahhhhh! A MOUSE!" I screamed as the mouse jumped out of the candy bag. "Mom!"

"What, Honey?" she answered.

"A mouse!" I said. "How are we ever going to catch it again?"

"Joey," my mother said, "go downstairs to get the doorman before I have a heart attack." So he did. (As fast as he could.)

"The doorman said to put peanut butter in a bag and the mouse will go into the bag and you will catch it," reported my brother.

That's exactly what we did. I'm surprised it worked, but indeed it did.

I just learned something. Mice like peanut butter.

Ask your students to think about what this piece might have looked like before the student revised it. Here's my guess as to how it read:

We saw a mouse in our apartment. My brother asked the doorman what we should do about it. He suggested that we put peanut butter into a brown paper bag. We did and we caught the mouse.

(This is a possibility. But when I spoke to this student about it at the time he wrote it, he said that the way it really happened is that they saw the bag moving and they quickly grabbed the end of the bag and rolled the edge to seal it. They brought it down in the elevator and handed it to the doorman.)

You might like to ask students what the author did to improve this piece. Some might say "The writer added dialogue." Others might say "The writer turned it into a story," or "The writer added action," or "It was more exciting." Of course, children are going to be itching to tell you their rodent stories, which is great for a few minutes, but don't let this sidetrack the lesson!

Students may also take a piece of well-known writing, such as a story they're all familiar with, and write what the first draft might have been like.

The famous example of this type of revising backward is the imaginary first draft of the Gettysburg Address by Abraham Lincoln:

Final Draft: Four score and seven years ago, our fathers brought forth upon this continent a new nation . . .

And here's Abe's first draft:

First Draft: Our first government was formed here about eighty-seven years ago . . .

Which one stirs the imagination?

Have children use a familiar folk tale to revise backward. For example, what would a first draft of Paul Bunyan look like? Kids might come up with something like this:

Paul Bunyan was very big and strong. He was about six feet tall. He was so strong that he could lift a 100-pound sack of flour easily. He could run a mile in about five minutes, and that's fast for such a big man.

That's a story that needs some work!

A Whole New Ball Game

It is important for children to work in different genres. This is a game that invites students to take samples of drafts in one literary genre and transform them into another genre.

Here's an example of descriptive prose about snowflakes:

Snowflakes come down from the heavy grey clouds. They are light. When the wind blows they swirl up again. The wind calms down and they fall down in soft, white layers on the ground.

Here's a different genre, a poem, written by a fourth grader about the same subject:

A Young Snowflake
by Sophia

As I drift down from father cloud
A gust of wind picks me up.
As he carries me along
I can see my brothers and sisters
pleasantly sitting on the ground beneath me.
The gust of wind lets me fall
and I slowly drift
to the ground
to sleep.

Invite children to write about the same subject matter in a variety of literary forms: a poem, a fictional story, a personal reflection, and a factual piece. Through this exercise, children learn that often there is a form that

seems especially right for their topic. For example, a walk home in the rain is probably more effective as a poem than a story; the year Grandmother lost the Thanksgiving turkey lends itself more to personal essay or short story. Students may discover that revising their pieces into a different genre is a pleasing way out of writer's block.

To wake up dull expository pieces, a teacher in my school did a "Facts about . . ." activity with her students, in which each child selected a topic, read reference books and took notes about it, and then put himself—or a personal voice of some kind—into his piece. For example, a student wrote an autobiography of an artic fox: "My life as an arctic fox is not easy, but at least the air is clean." Another student, Tom, turned his notes on

India into a fact-based account of a visit to India.

Tom has many stories about India. He might be a famous author someday. This is one story from a large collection of pieces about India that he is writing. Tom smoothly incorporates facts from reference books and facts that he knows from his own experience. I worked with him to help him focus his ideas into this story. He brought in the actual slingshot to show me. It is so strong and well made that I think it will last for many more years.

In his final draft, Tom has a livelier title and opening, and a stronger storyline.

How the sling shot was made

This kid made the sling shot with ruber from tiyer's and some strong stick's

About The kid

This kid is strong but he is poor. He could clime tree's good and he could swim to it is hard to klim thee's in India. The reson is that there are ants and they will bite you but it is ok for him.

by TOM

The Kid Who Made a Slingshot
by Tom, Grade 3

One day when I was in India in a little town in the country, my Dad and I started to go to the city to buy a slingshot. I wanted one so that I could go hunting and stuff. This kid who lived right across the bridge asked us, "Where are you going?"

My dad said that we were going to buy a slingshot for me. The kid said, "Don't go. They cost a lot of money. I will make it for you."

This kid is strong but he is really poor. He could climb trees very well and he could swim too. It is hard to climb trees in India. The reason is that there are ants and they will bite you but it is OK for him.

So he set off to work on it. This is how he made it. He cut rubber from old tires. He cut strips of rubber about one-half inch wide. He collected strong sticks. He tied the sticks together with the rubber. He fastened the end of the rubber to the sticks. You can put a rock in it and shoot it.

It was a really good slingshot. It has lasted for about three years.

CHAPTER 6

A Selection of Mini-Lessons for Revision

I would sometimes bring in my first draft to show my students…
I would tell them: You have to have a longing to make it good. If you
don't have the longing, you're not a real writer.
—Grace Paley

Children have a hard time revising in general. It is easier to revise in particular. They need clear-cut ideas to put into action immediately. It might be good to focus on one revision strategy for a few days, or even for a week or two. Here are some strategies that usually work well for second to sixth graders:

IDEAS FOR REVISING:

- ❁ **Create an opening that grabs attention.**
- ❁ **Add details.**
- ❁ **Change some verbs to action verbs.**
- ❁ **Use dialogue.**
- ❁ **Show how characters feel.**
- ❁ **Organize your paragraphs.**
- ❁ **Use figurative language.**

(See Chart 7 in the Appendix for a reproducible chart of this.)

Present each strategy separately one day, a few days, or a week at a time. These strategies can be especially effective as mini-lessons after most of your students have written their first drafts. A sample mini-lesson for each is provided for you to use as is, to expand into a few lessons, or to modify in any way that you see fit.

Each mini-lesson uses the outline below:

1. **Present a model.**

2. **Get kids to connect.**

3. **Explain the strategy.**

4. **Create a sample together.**

5. **Invite each student to apply this strategy to a current draft. (Share these at end of writing session.)**

These mini-lessons should be brief—not more than ten minutes. It is more important to provide motivation than anything else. Very often, however, the model and the discussion itself provide the motivation, because when children see what *can* be done, they immediately want to try it out. Because these are first-step lessons, I recommend that every student apply the strategy to his or her own writing. They do not have to keep the addition or change, but they at least have to come up with something in order to make a choice about their own writing. They shouldn't reject it before they even try it on for size. Experimenting in this way helps kids gain control over their work.

MINI-LESSON #1

Create an Opening that Grabs Attention

1. Present a model.

Read to your students the two passages below, written by James, grade 2:

DRAFT #1

I went to a cave last summer. It was awesome. I went with my family to a cave. When we came to a mouse sticking on the cavern wall, I thought it was a bat. Soon I saw a bat in a hole. Soon we went underground boating. So we went out of the cave.

DRAFT #2

"Yikes, what's that?" screamed Marie. Something had swooped down near my sister's head.

I went to a cave last summer. I went with my family. We kept on walking further into the cave. I was looking up. I saw this hole above. "What's that thing up there?" I asked. "It's kind of like a piece of stone, but I just saw it move. Maybe it's alive!" I saw it hanging upside down by its feet.

"That has to be a bat," said one of the kids on the tour.

The tour guide told us a story. A boy had a mouse in his pocket. The mouse jumped out and fell into the water. It bounced off the water and landed on the wall and froze.

Bats are not exactly like mice. Bats have wings and mice don't. Mice stay on the ground and bats hang from the cave.

This is one trip I will never forget. It was awesome!

---

2. Get kids to connect.

Ask students questions about the two drafts:

- ❀ What is the same and what is different about the two stories that I have just read to you?

- ❀ What did the second story have that the first one didn't?

- ❀ How were the first sentences different?

- ❀ Which story did you like better? Why?

3. Explain the strategy.

Through discussion, children realize that the second story is more effective because it grabs people's attention immediately. (It does this in a few ways, such as adding exclamations, dialogue, feelings, and tension. But at this point it is not a good idea to go through all of these or the mini-lesson will take too long. Each of these could be a mini-lesson by itself.)

Here's a simple and direct explanation of the strategy for your students:

> "In your writing create a beginning that will make a reader want to read more. You need to stir up some excitement. It's a lot of fun to do this. Think of ways to make your readers wonder what's going to happen next. Think of a detail that they will want to find out more about. Put them in the middle of the action. Consider using humor."

4. Create a sample together.

Ask for a student volunteer to read aloud the first paragraph or two of a story he is working on, and then invite the class to make suggestions for a stronger beginning. You may wish to have the writer make the first suggestion. In any event, it's helpful to have a note-taker record the suggestions for the student to take back and work with.

5. Invite each student to apply this strategy to a current draft. (Share these at end of writing session.)

Send students back to their writing by inviting all of them to try out a new beginning for one of their pieces.

Does my story beginning grab the reader? Third-grader Erick recorded it and replayed it to see how it sounds.

MINI-LESSON #2
Add Details

1. Present a model.

Read aloud each of the following stories:

1. The cat fell off the roof.

2. The little kitten was shivering. The ice storm caught it by surprise. It had climbed up onto the slate roof. It was hard to get a footing and it slid right off.

2. Get kids to connect.

Ask students for reactions to the two versions of the same story. Ask questions such as the following:

- ☀ What does the second story have that the first story does not?

- ☀ Which story helped you to form a picture of what happened?

- ☀ Which story was more fun to hear?

- ☀ Which story held your interest?

- ☀ Which story gave you more ideas?

In "Ghosts," below, Susan displays her ability to use sensory details. Susan's family came from Korea. She told me that she was only five when she went to Korea, so this story is one she remembers from two or three years before. She first wrote the draft in October and then revised it in May. You can see how much she grew as a writer.

DRAFT #1

Ghosts

by Susan

Some tims I make mastaks in school. In Kerea I felt cold and it was these goust that maked me cold. Wene I go to bed my feet were relly relley cold in the middle of the night.

FINAL DRAFT

Ghosts

by Susan

My name is Susan and I am eight years old. I was born in America.

One time I went with my mom and sister to Korea. My sister and I went to the play ground. I felt cold. There were two chosts that looked like the same. They looked funny. kThey khad big weird round hats. Teh ghosts were cold. They went right through me. It was these ghost that made me cold.

I ran away with my sister and told my mom that it looked funny then she laughed.

---

3. Explain the strategy.

The second version had more details. It helped us to picture exactly what was happening. It put us right at the scene of the action.

Add details—it's probably the best strategy to use when rewriting. Tell kids that when they revise, they should read the story over and think about what happened—or might have happened. Writing from real life helps you to do this because you can think about the way it really was. You can then tell about it in a very particular way—for example the detail of the "shivering kitten" was a good one because we could see it as if it were happening right in front of us. Think about what time of day it was, or what the weather was like. You might like to include any sounds or smells that might have been there. Sense details are important. Think about what things looked like and who was there. Do everything you can to bring your reader into the story.

4. Create a sample together.

Ask one of your students to share a current draft or to think of a story on the spot. Then ask for suggestions on how to make the story better by adding details. Write the suggestions on a chalkboard or chart. Review the results, and point out the benefit of adding details.

5. Invite each student to apply this strategy to a current draft. (Share these at end of writing session.)

Invite students to take out their current pieces and read them carefully. They should try to think of ways in which adding details can make their pieces of writing better. They should write a few of these details between the lines or in the margins of their drafts. Invite them to share these changes at the end of this writing session.

MINI-LESSON #3
Change Some Verbs to Action Verbs

1. Present a model.

Here's an example that you might like to write on the board or on a chart:

Jaime walked to school.

Say to your class, "Here's a plain old sentence. This sentence means just what it says, although it might make you wonder what's so special about this particular kid. How can we change the verb *walked* to a more interesting action verb?"

Accept several suggestions such as "hobbled," or "sauntered," or "trudged."

2. Get kids to connect.

Give them this sample of a piece of writing that has verbs that describe action and other conditions:

> "Morey was this old musician with skin like brown velvet. When the light shone on it, his skin gleamed gold. Most of the time he slopped around in an old flannel shirt and army fatigue pants . . ." (From *Child of the Owl* by Laurence Yep, HarperCollins, 1977.)

Discuss the work. You might say: "In this sample, there are some great verbs. Who can find them?" Accept *shone, gleamed*, and *slopped around in*. Discuss why these words are more effective than the words, *fell, looked*, and *wore*.

3. Explain the strategy.

Emphasize that the revision strategy of changing some dull, overused verbs to action verbs can help improve the writing by creating active events or by describing a mood or situation more precisely. Point out that children can look through their own work for dull verbs and change them to livelier ones.

4. Create a sample together.

Now, pass out a paper with very dull sentences on it (or ask the children to write their own dull sentences). They should allow plenty of space for revision. Ask students to change some of the tired verbs in the sentences to action verbs— verbs that create a colorful picture of the action. They can simply write the new verb above the old one. Talk about the results.

The Kids played ball after

Next, ask students to look at their own selection of verbs in a piece of writing and to be ready to discuss them. Ask for examples of how they can change some of the verbs to new, livelier ones. Make sure that they understand the basic idea, that is, that carefully chosen action words can make a piece of writing come alive. Put a few examples of dull words on the board. As a group, have students change them to bright words. Review the results.

Caution: Make sure that they don't

> **Make sure that students don't overdo the use of action verbs.**

overdo it—it can also become distracting. A good example of this is the overuse of action verbs instead of using *said*. *Said* can be a perfectly good word to attach a speaker to a piece of dialogue. But if other words are used for no reason, it becomes silly: "Hi," she exclaimed. "Hi, how are you?" he uttered. "I'm fine," she expressed. In a case like this, *said* is a reasonable, effective verb. Readers today appreciate a clear, direct style.

5. Invite each student to apply this strategy to a current draft. (Share these at end of writing session.)

You might like to say this: "Go back to your draft and use a colored pencil or thin marker and underline all of the verbs. Then try to think of other words that fit and that can communicate the action or condition in a vivid way. Write them down. Read the piece silently, using the new words instead of the old words. Cross out the ones you don't like. You might even like to keep the word you started with. Test the new word and then decide. Later I will ask you to share any changes you made."

Here's how Sophia, a fourth grader, used action words instead of *were* and and *went*:

The Gray City
by Sophia

As I stepped out of the cab I saw London, a murky, rainy city. Grey shadows of mysterious figures lurked around every corner. People walked silently with hat-covered faces along the damp streets. An occasional car zoomed past. Beautiful cathedrals and other buildings towered above my head.

I could smell the delicious smell of the ocean as I truged along the streets that smelled of wet dog. My family and I waved down a cab. When I stepped into the cab the aroma of plastic filled my nose.

As we drove along I could hear the sound of a rickety old engine rattling under me. When I got out of the cab I heard the honking of horns and sound of cars.

A truck zoomed past, I tried to jump out of the way but it was to late. The truck had drive through a deep puddle and I got soaked! I could feel the wettness on my coat. I wiped the hair out of my eyes and the wet from my hair got on to my hand

That is London.

MINI-LESSON #4
Use Dialogue

1. Present a model.

Here's an excerpt from a story by sixth grader Katie:

> "Paul, ya need some help with that?" I asked while my brother was carrying a big tractor engine.
>
> "No thanks, you wouldn't be any help anyway," he said rudely.
>
> "I hate you!!" I said. You're treating me like dirt! I'm going in the kitchen so I don't have to be treated bad by an idiot," I screamed at him.

I don't have a copy of her first draft, but it might have sounded like this:

> My brother drives me crazy. I try to be nice to him, and he is as nasty as ever. When he makes me feel stupid, I really lose my temper and start screaming at him.

2. Get kids to connect.

After reading both passages, generate a discussion with questions like these:

* ❋ Do you think that the dialogue helps the writing?

* ❋ How does dialogue tell us about how people treat each other?

* ❋ Can you tell us about the personality of the characters from the way they talk?

* ❋ Which passage is more immediate and real-life? (Which one feels more like you are actually there?)

3. Explain the strategy.

From this discussion you have already given children a good sense of how dialogue helps a story. If necessary, summarize these points for the class:

* ❋ When we record what people say to one another, we call it dialogue. The words must have quotation marks around them, and the speaker must be indicated.

⚜ Writers use dialogue to create the conversation as it happened, or, in the case of fiction, as you, the author, imagine the conversation to have happened. Yes, you can make up dialogue, but it works best when it sounds as close as possible to the way people actually talk. In our example, the author probably has heard a brother and sister arguing with each other like that, and she made it fit the action of the story.

4. Create a sample together.

Ask students, Who would like to give us an example of how you might revise your piece by adding some dialogue?

After students present a few examples, reinforce the idea that dialogue may enhance a story.

5. Invite each student to apply this strategy to a current draft. (Share these at end of writing session.)

Send the class back to revise their pieces by adding (or improving) dialogue.

MINI-LESSON #5
Show How Characters Feel

1. Present a model.

We are very familiar with the oft-assigned piece of writing from our own schooling: "What I Did on My Summer Vacation," or "My First Day of School."

The following piece is written on the latter topic, but shows plenty of feeling.

---

by Stephen, Grade 3

I thought on the first day of school you were going to turn out bad. But you turned out great! I was thinking about making no friends but I made seven friends.

This is a powerful little piece that expresses a child's fears before the first day of third grade and the relief that everything turned out okay. In three simple sentences, Stephen managed to convey authentic emotion—that's more than some published writers accomplish in a hundred pages!

Third-grader Maggie took a personal experience and created a charming story about a lupine bush. This is an example of a factual piece that nevertheless has a lot of warmth.

The Lupine Phases
by Maggie

At the end of the spring my dad bought me a beautiful little lupine bush in a little black pot. We let it grow in the little black pot. Then after a few days we planted it. All we needed to plant it was a shovel and dirt. In a few minutes it was in the moist ground. Then we went inside. A week later it looked like this. (It was supposed to be pink.)

In the meantime I went to school, did my homework, played with my friends, and slept. In about another week or so it grew taller and taller. Soon it budded little pink buds and crisp green leafs. In another two weeks the plant was full grown with the most delicate pink flowers ever.

The weeks and months went by and soon it was fall. The leaves dried and the flowers fell off and by winter my lupine was nothing but a stem.

Maybe in the spring my dad will buy me a purple lupine bush. If he does, I will write about it just like I did for my pink lupine bush.
The End

2. Get kids to connect.

Ask various questions to help your students appreciate the power of feelings in a piece of writing:

❊ What do you think about your two pieces?

❊ Which one was more personal? Why?

❊ Why do you think that the second piece was a stronger piece? What did it have that the first one didn't?

❊ How many different feelings were expressed in the second piece?

❊ Have you ever had any of these feelings?

3. Explain the strategy.

The strategy of showing how a character feels is not an easy one to use. Make sure that your students appreciate the difficulty before they begin so that they don't become discouraged if it doesn't work right way. Also, the key word is *show*. It's important to not just say, "He felt sad," but to convey the feeling in the situation—for example, "I was thinking about making no friends." The vulnerability and longing that is conveyed in those simple words is so much more powerful than the use of a word that tells a feeling, such as *sad* or *happy*. Stephen *showed* how he felt by bringing us into his inner thoughts and fears. He didn't just tell us.

4. Create a sample together.

Ask your students to review their pieces. Say: "Think of the situation that made you choose to write this story in the first place. It must have meant something to you. Try to figure out what it was about the situation that moved you—you might have been jealous, sad, worried, or thrilled. As you read your pieces, try to keep in mind that feeling. Then try to think of details that support that feeling. For example, if you felt depressed, you might want to mention that it was raining out and your room was a mess. If you want to express the guilt you felt when your mother discovered what you did, don't say you felt guilty. Try to think of a physical sensation or an expression you experienced—for example, 'The lump in my throat grew the longer my mother sat there and said nothing.' Would anybody like to give me an example from your own writing in which you show feelings?" Talk about the work. Write it on the board. Ask for ways to improve it even more, and have students do so as a group.

5. Invite each student to apply this strategy to a current draft. (Share these at end of writing session.)

Accept one or two examples, and then invite all of your students to immediately review their pieces for areas in which they can make revisions to show feelings. Sometimes this review might lead to a complete rewriting of the story. That's fine, because the feeling usually is the real story. Revision is about going deeper into one's writing, deeper into the emotional terrain surrounding the story's events.

Helping children realize the power of writing is one of the most valuable things we can do.

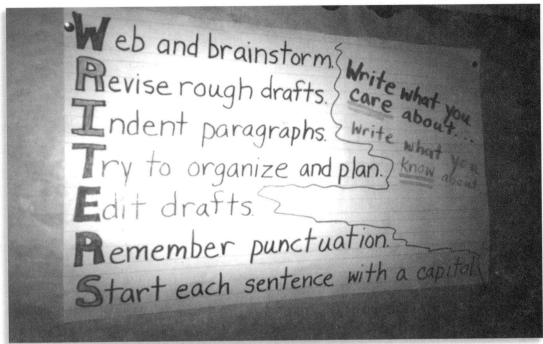

Third-grade teacher Vickie Wu Zazyczny created a chart to motivate—and guide—her students' revisions.

MINI-LESSON #6
Organize Your Paragraphs

1. Present a model.

Here's a first draft written by Justin, a fourth grader:

DRAFT 1

The Beaches of Cape Cod

I remember when I was in Cape Cod. The sand was so hot my feet nearly got on fire. When the waves hit the shore they made the shore rattle like an earthquake. The air was fresh and salty. The fishermen were casting their lines out and reeling all the fish in. I went over the shiny blue waves while swimming. The grey and white seagulls fly up above.

Justin's teacher asked him to take his water-based markers and highlight the different topics of his piece in different colors. He did that; he also added a few sentences. On the next page you'll find a later draft.

DRAFT #2

The Beaches of Cape Cod

I remember when I was in Cape Cod. The sand was so hot my feet nearly got on fire. *When the waves hit the shore they made the shore rattle like an earthquake.* **The air was fresh and salty.** <u>The fishermen were casting their lines out and reeling all the fish in.</u> *I went over the shiny blue waves while swimming.* <u>The grey and white seagulls fly up above.</u>

The air was so sweet . . . I could just about taste the air.

When the waves came in they just about knocked me over. The water was so cold it was like being in Antarctica. I thought I was crazy to go into the water.

Here's the final version.

DRAFT #3

The Beaches of Cape Cod

I remember when I was in Cape Cod.

The beach sand was so hot my feet nearly caught on fire. When the waves came in they almost knocked me over. The water was so cold, it was like being in Antarctica. I thought I was crazy to go into the water but I did. I went over the shiny blue waves while swimming.

The air was sweet and fresh. The air was so sweet it was like a breath of fresh air.

The fishermen were casting their lines out and reeling in all different size fish. The grey and white seagulls fly up above my head.

I think Cape Cod beaches are the best!

---

2. Get kids to connect.

After showing the drafts, do a quick review of what paragraphs are. Then, as a class, look carefully at drafts two and three. Ask the following:

☀ What is a paragraph?

☀ How short or long can a paragraph be?

☀ How do you know what sentences belong in a paragraph and what do not? Is it sometimes a judgment call? (That is, does it sometimes depend on the way you look at it? An example of this would be that all of the above could be thought of as only one paragraph, or it could be divided into additional paragraphs.)

❀ What do you think about the way Justin organized his paragraphs?

❀ Can organization into paragraphs improve a piece of writing?

3. Explain the strategy.

Discuss with students the following points:

❀ A paragraph is one or more sentences that make sense together. Paragraphs usually contain a single train of thought. Paragraphs are a way to organize a piece of writing so that it reads smoothly and logically.

❀ There are ways to plan paragraphs before you write. Many writers do this as they think and plan what they are going to write. They think of an outline and then write enough for each topic of the outline to complete and to give balance to the piece. An example of this would be the following:

Main Topic:	How To Bake Bread
#1	Why one does it
#2	What the process consists of
#3	How one feels about the results

The three subtopics may each be a paragraph long. The middle topic may be one paragraph, or it may be divided into a few—for example, gather and measure ingredients; mix and knead the dough; wait for the dough to rise; bake.

When we are reviewing our pieces to see if they need to be revised, it's a good idea to check for paragraphs and to see whether or not the sentences are grouped in a logical order. It is also a good idea to see if the sentences are arranged in a proper time sequence.

4. Create a sample together.

Duplicate an actual piece of student writing or one of your own pieces. It's very effective to use a transparency and an overhead projector for this. Choose a piece that is obviously not in paragraph form and that might have various scattered topics. Highlight the similar topics with the class. Discuss the fact that when the piece is rewritten, it can be written with the proper paragraphs.

5. Invite each student to apply this strategy to a current draft. (Share these at end of writing session.)

Ask students to carefully review their current drafts. Invite them to look for single topics that might go together and highlight each with a different color marker. Then, when rewriting the draft, arrange the topics to go into appropriate paragraphs. Indicate that you would be glad to hear about any single topics that they are able to find that could become separate paragraphs.

MINI-LESSON #7
Use Figurative Language

1. Present a model.

In children's literature, there are many superb examples of the use of figurative language. Here is one of my favorites:

> "It was an old photograph, fading away like a dawn that leaves you little by little, and it was of a child." (from *Missing May* by Cynthia Rylant, Dell, 1992).

Share several examples from books, as well as from student work. Here, fourth-grader Perri shows her flair for writing similes:

```
The cool water touched my feet like hands.
```

2. Get kids to connect.

The use of figurative language intensifies the effect of the story on the reader. That is because the figure of speech produces a complex effect—it startles, it delights, it causes the memory to go into the active mode, it causes the reader to make associations, it moves the reader by its aptness and even by its beauty, it recreates for the reader the same experience that the writer had.

Discuss the effect that some of the samples had on your students. Ask questions such as the following:

❂ How can water be like hands?

❂ How can a fading photograph be like "a dawn that leaves you little by little"?

✿ Do you get a kick out of these ways of writing?

✿ How can you do this to your own writing?

3. Explain the strategy.

Explain the following to your students:

When we write we can think about new and better ways to express the same thought. We can use various figures of speech such as metaphors, similes, and oxymorons. (Metaphors and similes are comparisons in which one object is likened to another. A metaphor does not use *like* or *as*, whereas a simile does. An oxymoron is a combination of incongruous words.) In general, we call this figurative language. Poets and other writers often use it.

Examples:

Metaphor: My knees were jelly.

Simile: His speech is as smooth as silk.

Oxymoron: He showed cruel kindness.

When we want to express a thought using figurative language, we might just think of something to compare that thought to. An example of this would be to express your reaction to being embarrassed by saying, "I wished that the ground would swallow me up."

It's a lot of fun to make up these comparisons. Often they come out naturally in your first draft as you compose your piece. But sometimes you need to think hard about how to add figurative language that really works to make the writing clearer and more powerful.

4. Create a sample together.

Ask for examples of figurative language from your students' current drafts. Then invite one of your students to share a sentence that does not contain figurative language. (If no one wants to volunteer, someone may simply make one up on the spot.) Ask the group for possible ways to improve that sentence by adding a figure of speech such as a simile—for example, "I swung the bat and the ball flew through the air *like* . . . ." Children can supply all kinds of ideas: like it had wings; like a white dove, and so on. Now revise the sentence with kids to see if you can use figurative language to convey the character's state of mind. For example, "I swung that bat like it was bottom of the ninth in the World Series, and thousands of fans were at the edge of their seats." Remind kids that figurative language isn't just pretty window dressing; when it works best, the imagery helps reveal a narrator's or a character's feelings.

Perri was working with her teacher on using sense details and imagery in this piece about Cape Cod. She did about five drafts of this piece. Here is one of the early drafts and the final copy. The main difference is in the organization of the paragraphs.

EARLY DRAFT

Cape Cod

by Perri

When I got out of my family's boat, the green Fram, the cool water touched my feet like hands.

The first thing I saw when I looked down was the graygreen water with the slimy rocks on the bottom. When I looked up there was the big yellow sun in the blue sky.

When I looked onto the land I saw again the grey green water, washing up the white shells onto the tan sand whith the green dune grass.

I went ashore the sand was hot under my feet. The air smelled like salt.

I could faintly hear the big waves crashing up on the other far shore. The seagulls flying overhead teasing me. I walked to the other beach swam, came back and got on the boat and went home on gliding swiftly through the water.

FINAL DRAFT

Cape Cod

by Perri

When I got out of my family's boat, the green Fram, the cool water touched my feet like hands.

The first thing I saw when I looked down was the gray-green water with the slimy green rocks on the bottom. When I looked up there was the big yellow sun in the blue sky.

When I looked onto the land I saw the grey-green water, washing the white shells onto the tan sand with the green dune grass.

I went ashore the sand was hot under my feet. The air smelled like salt. I could faintly hear the big waves crashing up on the far shore. The seagulls crying to see if we had any food. I walked to the far shore. Swam came back and got on the sail boat and went home gliding swiftly through the seaweed strewn water.

5. Invite each student to apply this strategy to a current draft. (Share these at end of writing session.)

Send children back to their writing with the goal of looking over their draft and doing two things:

1. Look for any figurative language that you have already used, and put a check mark next to it.

2. Look for any possible places in your draft where figurative language might strengthen the effect on the reader. Try out a few possibilities and choose one. Insert it into the draft. (Be sure to remind them not to overdo it, or it will sound like a writing assignment instead of a heartfelt piece of writing.)

At the end of the writing time, share examples and comment on them.

CHAPTER 7

Use Fun Strategies to Get Kids to Revise

When we finish our story, or a few days or weeks later, we must stand far enough back from our work to feel ourselves no longer the author, but the reader and the critic; to work to some point of indifference where it will seem the story has been written by someone other than ourselves.

—Hallie and Whit Burnett, *The Fiction Writer's Handbook*

We have already examined and perhaps tried out ways to let children know what models of revision look like, and we've given specific examples of the kinds of revision one can do with a mini-lesson for each type. Now it's time to develop ways of helping students get some distance from their writing pieces. Usually, it's very easy for children to see in other people's writing what changes have to occur; it's very difficult to see one's own writing objectively enough to be able to know what should be revised.

Here are some strategies that will help students see their own writing through the eyes of others.

Goldfish Bowl Conference

Good conferencing can lead to good revising. The writers' conference is usually a private activity in which the writer reads the piece aloud to the partner, whether it is a teacher or another student, and the partner listens carefully. Then the partner reacts to the piece by commenting and by asking questions that help the writer think about the piece.

Third-graders Mathew and Sarah conduct a goldfish bowl conference.

The goldfish bowl conference is a powerful motivator and model. It is based on the group-dynamics technique of modeling an interaction. It is a public way to let students witness a private conference. This can be done by pretending that the conference is taking place as usual except that the partners are inside an imaginary goldfish bowl. All or some of the students in the class are invited to see the conference right through the bowl. The conference progresses as if the audience weren't there, yet they benefit from seeing and hearing a model of what a real conference is like.

Children I have taught love the goldfish bowl conference. Of course, the two conference partners must be volunteers. The hardest job falls to the conference partner who needs to ask the right questions, for they make all of the difference in whether or not the conference is productive. Effective questions inspire rather than discourage the writer, and help the writer to discover how to revise the piece.

At this point I recommend that you post the chart "Questions for Writers—Try Some!" (see the Appendix) to guide children in conducting the goldfish bowl conference. (For younger children, you might like to use only three or four questions.)

The goldfish bowl strategy is different from a group conference in a subtle but important way. It maintains the sense of privacy and intimacy of a one-to-one conversation, because the conference partners pretend there is no one listening. And for the audience, listening is a powerful experience; it's as though the children are watching a play, or eavesdropping. They hang on— and learn from—every word.

This brings us to another effective strategy for revision: role-playing.

Role-Playing

*A*ny strategy that helps students to have some distance from what they have just written is useful. Second through sixth graders love to play roles—that is, they love to try on other personalities that differ from their own.

The Teacher

An obvious role for a student to play is that of the teacher. This becomes most effective if there is a mimic in the group—a child who is particularly good at imitating your gestures, speech inflections, and so forth, for the group. The kids rock with laughter when this happens, and the lesson on revision that you want to get across will never be forgotten. Here's an example of the dialogue that might occur:

> "Now children. Listen carefully. You need to hook your reader. Where's my hook? I had it just a while ago. Did anyone see my hook? Did anyone see my glasses? Did anyone see what I did with that piece of chalk? Well, let's get back to working on making your writing better. Hook your reader with a joke. Take my piece of writing. Please." From one side of the room, a big hook comes out and pulls the teacher offstage.

Role-playing the teacher can be done in a straight way as well. The writer may read his piece to his partner as usual. Then the partner can role-play the writer, and the writer can role-play the teacher. The writer can ask the questions that he thinks the teacher would actually ask. (See the suggestions on page 26, Chapter 3.)

This can create a bit of distance and fun. The partner should answer the questions about the piece as if he or she were the other student. These answers—whether about lead paragraphs, character motivation, setting, or the basic idea of the story—can jolt the writer into seeing his work in a whole new way.

Here's an example of what the dialogue might sound like:

> *"Teacher"* (a student pretending to be the writer): What part works the best for you?

> *Student* (pretending to be the writer of the piece): Well, I like the part about how my dog jumped into the lake.

> *"Teacher"*: Why do you like that part?

> *Student*: Because he showed how brave he was.

> *"Teacher"*: I'd like to hear more about that dog.

> *Student*: Okay. I can tell you plenty about him.

The Professional Critic

Prepare children for this strategy by reading some professional book reviewers' pieces. It's probably best not to use really negative reviews as models, although that can also create some fun if this type of review is so preposterous that it is funny. Look for reviews of juvenile literature, especially of books that students are familiar with. The school librarian can help you locate a few.

Ask children to review their own writing that is still in process by role-playing the professional reviewer or critic. They can get into the role by giving themselves a name and by trying to give real reactions to the writing as if they were a real reviewer. This is not easy, but there are usually a few children who will get into it. They should give a catchy title to their review that might play on the actual title of the piece. For example, if the title of the piece is "The Day I Fell in Love at Coney Island," the professional critic, I. M. Wright, might use this headline: "Fall in Love With This Story."

Use of Props

*T*he use of props can enhance role play. In fact, a hook (such as an umbrella handle) is a great prop. A hook can be used as a dramatic reminder to write a revised opening that better hooks the interest of the reader.

Chairs can be used as props to help the writer obtain distance from his or her own piece. The writer can read the piece to the partner. Then the writer can sit in the partner's chair and ask the questions while the partner sits in the writer's chair. Later, the partner, who has simply been listening, can give feedback to the writer.

Hats can also be used as props. If one is writing about an event that actually occurred, it might be helpful if he or she gets into being a reporter for a newspaper and wearing a reporter's hat—a fedora with a press ticket in the brim. A lively reporter can inject some action into a tired piece.

A camera is an excellent way to demonstrate what it means to focus on the key idea of a piece, rather than write about a lot of different things. Back in the early 1980s, I attended a presentation of the writing-process approach to writing and I still remember the camera that the presenter brought with her. Ever since then I have connected the writing process with the prop of the camera, and I have used it to explain the concept of focus to children.

Hand Puppets

Children of all ages get a kick out of hand puppets. They engage the imagination and can create a bit of distance between the student and his or her work, and lessen the self-consciousness the child might feel when talking about his or her work.

Third-grade teacher Lynette Pantale uses a hand puppet to make revision suggestions for Sonya.

Use any available hand puppet, or simply use a sock with two buttons for eyes. Put your hand in the sock. Manipulate the mouth by putting your thumb in the heel of the sock and the rest of your fingers in the toe of the sock. Make the hand puppet talk with your own voice. Here's a possible scenario:

Hi kids! My name is Bookie the Worm (or Arthur the Author, or Rita the Writer). I'm here to encourage you to look carefully at your piece of writing and to help you to figure out what you can do to make your writing better.

Joey, would you read your piece to me? (Joey reads a short piece aloud. All of the students are listening.) Wow, you're really beginning to sound like an author! If fact, you *are* an author. Authors write and then think about how they can make the piece even better. What do you think you need to add or change?

Pretend that you didn't write this piece and are hearing it for the first time. Read it aloud again. (Joey reads it again.) Was it clear? Did it tell a story that makes sense? Do you like what you've written? Now do you have any ideas about what you need to add or change?

A puppet conference partner can be great fun!

You can also do a little scene with two puppets having a conference about their own writing. Their conversation can be a model for students about how a conference can work. Any humor you can bring to this can give children an experience that they won't forget. Remember, fun is a great motivator.

Create a Character

*Y*ou may choose to use a standard character every time you give a lesson on revision. This character may function the way the characters Ms. Frizzle (Magic School Bus series) or Mr. Wizard (of TV fame) do in science. It is an immediately identifiable and likable attention-getter and focus person for the task at hand.

Patrick, the Revision Detective, at work.

Here's an example of such a character—the Revision Detective! All you need is a trench coat and a hat, or a Sherlock Holmes hat (a deerstalker) and pipe. And of course a magnifying glass! The Revision Detective is a master at looking for clues to what's at the core of a piece of writing

The Revision Detective says the following:

"With crooked politicians you follow the money trail; with writing you follow the feeling trail."

"Look closely at your writing—where is the part that grabs you? It might be a startling idea that excites you. It might be a sad episode that is very moving. It might be a totally hilarious event that makes you laugh every time. Focus on and develop that idea. That's the best revision you can do."

"Don't think that the reader is all-knowing. You've got to explain some things."

"Your writing must be clear to the reader, and you can't always limit the audience to only those in the know. Reread your piece to your conference partner, and see if there is any part that is not clear."

"Take your magnifying glass and see if you can find any run-on sentences or repeated words. Then eliminate them."

You can make a deerstalker hat from heavy paper (see photo) or by simply placing two baseball caps together with visors facing opposite directions.

Style can help clarity of writing. Although proofreading may take place only if you decide to publish your piece, sometimes working with the Revision Detective can stir up some excitement that makes you want to take it through to publication.

The Revision Detective is also great in helping kids find their usage and spelling errors when their piece is ready for final editing. (See Chapter 8, "When and How to Polish and Edit.")

Videotape a Conference

*T*he most important tool we have for revision is the conference, yet we need to show children how to conference effectively. Creating videotapes of students asking helpful questions, and of students reading aloud finished work that reflects conference suggestions, is a powerful motivator. (And yes, sometimes videos can even be a model of how *not* to do a conference.) Create a library of videos kids can check out and watch independently.

Audiotape a Conference

*C*hildren can audiotape their conferences. An audiotape is less of a distraction than a videotape and can always be used without a third person as an operator. Children become comfortable with it very quickly and often forget that it is there. When this happens, they will make a very natural audiotape.

Later, other children can listen to the audiotaped conferences. They are excellent examples for the rest of the class of what a conference is like. Then you will be able to walk them through the steps of how a writer can take the ideas from a conference and use them to revise the piece.

Audiotaping is also a useful tool for keeping students on task during a conference, for there is a great temptation for some children to talk at random and lose their concentration. These children get a great deal out of hearing how their fellow students take conferences seriously.

Allow a Piece to Age

*O*f course, one of the best ways for a writer to gain distance from a piece is to let it be for a while—a few weeks, a few months, or in the case of second grader Josh, a full year.

Josh chose his own topic, and it is an unusual one for a second grader. He wrote the first draft in second grade, and I saved it because I loved it. Then I asked him to revise it when he was in third grade. I was amazed at how free he was about changing the details. He had plenty of distance and was very free and easy about revising it. (See page 80.)

FIRST DRAFT

Facts About Stress

by Josh, Grade 2

There are many things that lead to stress. Mostly games. They can be board games, and card games and things like that. You can also get it at sports games.I have an example, say that you were at a soccer game. You were voting for your favrite team, the score was 0–1, and the other team was winning. It was the last qurter, there were five seconds left in the game! Do you feel sweaty? I would think so. Stress occurs at other sports, like: football, tennis, baseball, basketball, and lots more. You get stressfull when you really want something to happen but there is not much time for it to happen.

FINAL DRAFT

Facts About Stress

by Josh, Grade 3

Stress is one thing you run into many times in your life, even as a kid. There are many things that lead to stress, mostly games. They can be sports, board games, card games, and things like that. You can get stressful when you would like something to happen but you have a doubt that it can. Here's an example.

Say you're watching a New York Knick's game. It's the final game of the Championships. The Knicks are down by one point. The Knicks have the ball down at their court, three seconds left. Then Ewing gets fouled. It's a one-shop foul. If he makes the shot, they go into overtime. If not, the game is over. If you're a Knicks fan, you'd be pretty stressed out at that point. Do you feel sweaty? I would think so. Are you jumping up and down? Probably. Is your heart beating twice as fast?

That's what happens with stress.

Peer Teaching

There are numerous examples above of strategies that incorporate peer teaching techniques into the writing process. Every student-to-student conference is an example of peer teaching.

You can make the exercise of peer teaching more deliberate and more

Sixth-graders Howard and George have a peer conference.

explicit by setting up peer-teaching opportunities for specific students with a small group or in a one-on-one structure. They can also work with younger students.

The topic for the sessions is how to revise. The overall goal is to help the children to know what doesn't work in their writing and to fix it. This has to be done in a down-to-earth, positive atmosphere where there's a lot of give-and-take and a lot of risk-taking. (See Chapter 2.)

Develop a core group of two or three students who have good people skills, and train them in good questioning techniques. Then have them circulate and listen to children who are ready to read their pieces aloud. They then ask open-ended questions to really get the writers talking about their ideas. They can even give suggestions, knowing well that it is up to the individual student to decide what and how to revise the piece and whether they choose to revise it at all.

The core group of peer teachers can be available on assigned days. It is important that they also have time to do their own writing. On the assigned days, it might be a good idea to find another time during which they might do their own writing undisturbed. It is also important that they understand that the peer teaching helps them, too. It can encourage them to see the connections between the conference and the revision, and it can help them appreciate the struggle that some students have with writing and with not giving up.

Peer Revisers

There are many writers, amateur and professional, who like to write and are even good at writing, but who resist revising their own work. These writers often have a trusted colleague, a friend, or sometimes even a professional editor do their revising for them. They often can return the favor when their friend has a piece of writing that needs revision. The reviser may work on the piece by himself or herself and discuss the suggested changes with the writer later.

The key word is trust, for the writer must trust the reviser or it will be a wasted exercise. Certainly there can be disagreement, and there might even have to be discussion about the piece by both parties, but the writer must trust the reviser and value the suggestions. It is still up to the writer to incorporate the suggestions, but at least there is an openness to do that and a sense that the reviser is supporting the efforts of the writer.

The reason why this works so well is that it immediately puts distance between the writer and the piece of writing. This distance can keep the writer from being discouraged or feeling like a failure if he or she doesn't quite get it right the first time around. The distance can also give the writer the benefit of a fresh look from someone else's perspective.

Peer revisers can work in the classroom quite well with some children. Every child is different, and every student needs to use the strategy that works best for him or her. In an elementary classroom, you should give students a broad array of strategies and let them become comfortable and proficient with each before limiting them to one or two.

A peer reviser should be chosen by the individual student, although that does not always work. The choice is often influenced by who the child's friends are, rather than by who would be the most helpful reviser. It would be great if the peer revisers could revise each other's pieces because this keeps the process on a level platform. If that is not possible, try to make the best possible matches or arrangements.

CHAPTER 8

When and How to Polish and Edit

Omit needless words.

—Strunk and White, *The Elements of Style*

What is Editing?

Editing is a type of revision. Generally speaking, professional editors edit in two stages. First, they make suggestions to the author for revision of a manuscript, marking sentences that aren't clear, sections or chapters that need to be condensed, characters that need developing, and so forth. Once the author finishes revising, the editor does a final edit, tightening language, making sure the writing flows well, and correcting punctuation.

In the classroom, when we refer to editing as part of the steps of the writing process, we usually think of it as the last stage before making a final copy for publishing. Editing is the step that does not usually change the content of the piece; it usually corrects the piece for conciseness, accurate spelling and usage.

Questions and Answers About Editing

How does a writer know that it is time to edit?

When a writer has written a piece, has had one or more conferences about the piece, and has made any revisions to the piece that he or she wants to, it should be ready for editing. Any piece that will be brought to the final copy, or publishing, stage must be edited. There are pieces that the writer prefers to keep in draft form. These pieces may be completed and revised in the future, but for now they simply stay in the folder that contains drafts-in-progress.

> *Only select pieces get edited.*

How do we edit?

The way to edit is easier said than done; the way to edit is to look for mistakes and correct them.

What do we look for when we edit?

The hardest thing for some students to do is to recognize their errors. Here are some steps that students can take:

1. If you are unsure of the standard spelling of any word, circle that word.

2. Make sure that every sentence begins with a capital letter and ends with a period, question mark, or exclamation point. Dialogue should contain quotation marks.

3. Break up long, run-on sentences.

4. Eliminate unnecessary words, add missing words, and avoid repetition.

These steps may be incorporated into an Editing Check worksheet to be used for each piece that is edited. (See Worksheet 1 in the Appendix.)

To see the power of editing, look at sixth-grader Katie's piece on page 85. She chose the topic for persuasive writing in her writing class. The first draft and the final copy are different in significant ways. Notice the editing that she did. Katie organized her piece to make her points in a clearer way. The ending is improved. In the final copy, her argument is made directly to the reader.

How do we use our editing partners?

Invite students to choose a fellow student to read and review their piece. Remind them to choose someone who will do a good job. This may or may not be a friend. They may want to switch each time and edit the partner's piece of writing in return. Some teachers assign editing partners so that everyone gets an equal chance and so that problems don't arise between certain personalities.

Each student must do his or her own editing first, using the same list of what mistakes to look for. The editing partner should treat the draft with respect and should sign and date the Editing Check worksheet. This becomes an indicator for the teacher that the piece was edited and coedited.

FIRST DRAFT

Why You Should Wear a Helmet While Rollerblading
by Katie

Rollerblading is a fun sport. It can't be a fun sport if you don't have protection which can cause ~~a result of~~ painful injuries. Another thing you need to do to have fun is to have the proper protection. A helmet is most important. A person without using a helmet could severely injure ~~there~~ his head causing a cuncusion. The most important thing you need to rollerblade is confidence. Confidence to believe in yourself.

Wearing a helmet while rollerblading is very important. It not only can injure you it can leave your memory completely blank. Wearing a helmet can set a very good example for kids. Wearing a helmet doesn't just protect your head but its also a law. it is

Rollerblading is a very popular sport. Everyone all over the world Rollerblades and think about all the people not wearing a helmet. Think about all the people who a falling or getting serious injuries.

FINAL DRAFT

Why You Should Wear a Helmet While Rollerblading
by Katie

Rollerblading is a fun sport. It can't be a fun sport if you don't have protection which can cause painful injuries. The most important piece of equipment is a helmet. Wearing a helmet is a law in most states.

Think about if you didn't use a helmet and you get a serious injury, that can even be permanent. The consequence might be that you may never be able to rollerblade again. You only have one life so take care of it.

The most important thing you have to have to rollerblade is confidence. Confidence that you can do it, to believe in yourself.

This is why you need a helmet. Rollerblading is fun. If you have to wear a helmet think about how much better it is than to worry about hurting yourself.

What editing marks should we use?

Professional editing marks are a useful shorthand for our students to use. Here are the most common and easy ones. (See Chart 9 in Appendix.)

EDITING MARKS:	EXAMPLES:
Capitalize	≡
Add a word or words	∧
Omit a word or words	ℓ
Add a period	⊙
Add a comma	⌃⸴
Start a new paragraph	¶
Correct the spelling	sp. ◯

Some teachers ask that, if children are unsure of the standard spelling of any word, they circle that word as they write. Later, they can go back and look up the words in the dictionary to find the correct spellings.

What manipulatives can be used as editing tools?

To make an impression on your students, and to put some fun into what some students feel is a dreary task, various manipulatives can be used to make editing marks and reminders for editors.

1. **Colored paper clips**—A clip can be used to mark where a new paragraph should begin or where an inserted paragraph should be. A red clip may mean that you need to add a title to your piece; a green clip may mean that you need to write a concluding sentence or paragraph. You may wish to standardize the color-coding of the various clips.

2. **Pressure-sensitive dots**—A dot may be placed next to each misspelled word. Dots may be used on the Editing Check worksheets after each task is completed. Again, various purposes may be served by various colors.

3. **Colored markers or colored pencils**—Color can add some excitement to the editing process. The editing marks may be written in color and the words to be spelled may be circled in color.

4. **Cards**—Number cards (say from 1–10) may be clipped to a draft, indicating the sequence of paragraphs before the final copy is made. For example, if a child wants to reorganize her work, she can clip cards with a "1" next to all sentences intended for paragraph 1 in the revised work, and cards with a "2" for all sentences intended for paragraph 2.

5. **Stamps**—Rubber stamps with various words and sayings on them can be a great editing help. The most important one might be, "Needs editing." Stamps can be a quick way to indicate the most common editing needs: "Start all sentences with a capital," "Punctuate the end of a sentence," and "Check spelling."

CHAPTER 9

Portfolios that Record and Celebrate the Revision Process

Teachers need to understand how children become conscious of what they are doing. The edge of consciousness is the teaching edge for the craftsperson. It is the point where children are most aware of what they need to solve on the way to satisfying their intentions in writing.

—Donald H. Graves, *Writing: Teachers & Writers at Work*

The teacher who is interested in revision is the teacher who is interested in helping students grow as writers. The greatest evidence of a student's growth as a writer can be found in a well-constructed portfolio consisting of carefully selected examples of that student's writing.

Portfolios are assessment tools that allow students, parents, teachers, and administrators to see educational progress and growth over time. Portfolios are especially useful in assessing writing because they are process oriented, not product oriented. The writing process is revealed when one can see the first drafts and the revisions that followed.

Contents of the Writing Portfolio

The Writing Portfolio should include the following:

1. Selected pieces of finished writing

THE SELECTION PROCESS

The pieces may be selected by the student and/or the teacher, but some type of selection must take place. A portfolio is not simply a folder with all of the writing that a student has done for a certain time period.

I advise that students be given some part in the selection process. Because they do not always know which pieces to select, and because they often choose the

Sally shares her writing portfolio with the principal, Dr. Tully.

piece that might not be the most well written but might have the most emotional connection for them, some teachers are reluctant to allow students to choose the pieces for the portfolio.

Since students should have ownership of their own writing process, they should indeed have input into the choice. Some teachers solve the dilemma by having the teacher choose one piece and the student choose another. Whatever happens, you need to set up clear criteria for the choice. These criteria can be the basis of some mini-lessons. For students to make a good choice, they need to be taught the basis upon which good choices are made. They should also understand the reasons for the teacher's choice.

CRITERIA FOR THE CHOICE OF FINISHED WRITING

The following are some possible criteria that can be used for personal-experience writing, fiction writing, or expository writing. (See Worksheet 2 in the Appendix.)

Portfolio Criteria

⊛ The writing piece is complete, presentable, and well organized.

⊛ The writing is clear.

⊛ The writing flows.

⊛ The writing is appropriate for the audience.

⊛ The purpose is fulfilled.

⊛ The subject matter is important to the writer.

⊛ Qualities of good writing are evident.

⊛ The writing expresses the material creatively.

It is possible that not all of these criteria will be fully met, but at least there is evidence of them in some way. For students to make a choice based on these criteria, they must be actively engaged in the writing process. The revision process, in particular, gives them the objectivity and skills they need to be able to make the choice intelligently.

Some teachers, especially those of older children, prefer to have different criteria for different types of writing. That is perfectly fine.

2. Drafts that show any revisions that were made

The drafts are excellent artifacts that can document growth in a young writer. They can show in one glance what many paper-and-pencil tests barely show, that is, what steps the student has taken to improve as a writer. All of the strategies described in earlier chapters can help a student to develop the skills necessary for this. The portfolio can be a tribute to the hard work of the student.

Because of the increased use of word processing programs, students don't often have their drafts because the improvements were immediately entered on the screen and saved as a file. The computer thus removes a lot of the tedious rewriting that often has to be done. It is also a great motivator for young writers. In an effort to document growth in writing, it might be a good idea to ask students to save and print out some sample drafts.

3. Statements and letters showing student reflection

It is important for the student to select one or more pieces for the Writing Portfolio. It is just as important for the student to reflect on why the piece or pieces were selected. Various forms may be prepared to remind the student to reflect on each piece of writing. If this is done for each piece, it might very well make the next step in the selection process easier.

The most common form for student reflection is a letter to the teacher and/or parent, stating the reasons for the selection. This can be prepared according to the Portfolio Criteria list on the previous page.

In addition, an overview reflection may be included along these lines:

How I have grown as a writer

How I have met my goals in writing

What I need to do next

4. Reader response

Having a Reader's Response form (see Worksheet 5 in Appendix) or blank sheets for the reader of a Writing Portfolio to write comments, ask questions, or give reactions is an optional part of the portfolio, but I highly recommend it. This reinforces the message that we always write for an audience and that writing is communication. It is also a superb way to document the number of readers and to indicate the identities of the readers. Students may not only treasure their own writing in the portfolio, but the reader responses that are placed there as well.

The Revision and Assessment Connection

*T*he type of student reflection that is required by a Writing Portfolio is directly connected to the process of revision. In fact, the very same mental activity that is needed for revision is also needed to assess one's writing for the portfolio. It requires writers to be their own literary critics. They need distance from their own writing to such an extent that they can read a piece as if someone else had actually written it. They can then ask themselves, "Can I, this reader, see this piece of writing for what it is, with all of its limitations and possibilities for improvement?" or "What are its strengths and limitations?" This is an assessment activity.

This is exactly what revision requires, and the revision skills need to be taught as children are writing. As they build their skills, they become better revisers and, therefore, better writers.

Celebrating the Writing Process

You may want to plan ways to celebrate the writing that your students have done. Many teachers have displays of children's work, an Authors' Tea or a Writers' Breakfast to which parents and relatives are invited to hear children read their pieces, and all kinds of publications that honor children's writing.

Portfolios may also be celebrated. A portfolio exhibit, in which all of the component parts of the portfolio may be displayed and shared, is an excellent way to do this. Professional authors may be invited to share their own work as writers

An elegant Authors' Tea includes sharing the writing that children have done.

and to hear about and see the children's work. School district administrators and school board members may wish to participate in reviewing the Writing Portfolios.

The key element in all of this is to give recognition to our students for the fine writing that they have done and to mark this milestone in their growth as writers.

CHAPTER 10

My Reflections

It is fascinating to write a book about writing and to reflect on oneself as a writer while doing it. As I write, I have been aware of all of the revisions that I've been making on this manuscript. Sometimes I revise sentence by sentence and paragraph by paragraph. Sometimes I revise after a whole chapter. It is hard work and it takes quite a bit of time. What has governed the revision process from the very beginning is the sense of who the audience is, in this case teachers who are teaching writing, and what the focus is—revision. I think that young writers, too, have to have a clear idea of who their audience is and what their focus is. This will help them to know why and to what end the revisions are needed.

I have also been aware that I've learned a lot as I have written. I did not sit down at my computer each day knowing exactly what the content would be. "Write what you know" is a classic rule for good writing. But I wrote about things I know well, and about things I wanted to learn more about. Writing to discover what I didn't know that I knew sounds like a contradiction, but it's not. Discovery takes a great deal of foreknowledge. Before discovery, questions need to be asked. Questions arise from what one knows and from the gaps in one's knowledge. As we try to answer the questions and find solutions to the problem, it's amazing how ideas and clarity emerge.

This book began with a problem—with some gaps. The problem was one that didn't have a ready answer and that produces a lot of frustration in practice: How do I get my students to work on their writing by revising what needs to be revised? Knowing kids as teachers do, they know that most kids like to put closure on the task as soon as they come up with a passable piece. This even happens when they love to write and are taken with the topic. It's still extremely hard to get them to step back, look at their own writing, and make it better.

This problem has plenty of partial solutions. I've written books before and I always did a lot of revising of those works, but for my students, revision was often just one step of the writing process that they had to accomplish. By continuing to question and figure out some practical ways of teaching revision, I discovered a more effective approach.

The strategies suggested in this book are not new. They are, however, presented in a new way, or in a distinct context. In preparing for this book, I tried out some strategies at length, and some only briefly. Sometimes I made a satisfying improvement in my writing. Sometimes there was only a word or two added or a new title written at the top of the draft. The teachers with whom I've shared the manuscript in process have tried out various strategies suggested and they have reported some good results.

I still have some questions about the revision process.

Why are children so good about critiquing and giving feedback to their peers, yet so blind about their own pieces?

Of course, self-criticism is always hard, but I have a feeling that the blindness comes from the difficulty that kids have in getting some distance from their writing. It also might be willful—it's hard work to revise.

How can we reach the student who resists writing?

These are the students who not only won't revise, but they struggle with getting anything on paper. Venture a solution

How can we teach a student how to have and develop his or her own unique voice in the writing?

Young children have such a distinctive voice of their own. As they get older, many lose it. Donald Graves writes about the recurring loss and finding of that voice as a child goes from one developmental stage to the next. We recognize its charm and uniqueness when it's there. How do we make it happen if it's not there?

I have not solved the problem of revision. But I think that I have pointed to a direction in which we educators need to go. We need to help our students to see for themselves what needs to be done. At one point in the process, they need to stop being authors and to become readers and critics of their own work. The ball is placed in their hands during a conference on their writing; they need to take the ball and run with it.

I asked one of the second-grade classes in my school what advice they might give to a classmate who just had a conference and was reluctant to get back to work on the piece. Casey raised her hand and said, "Tell them, 'Never give up on your writing.'" The kids nodded in agreement. They thought that it would be great to make a banner for the hallway with these words so that the whole school could benefit. We did just that.

These strategies can be useful steps toward helping children grow as writers. There are many factors that influence the ability of a student to write in such a way that it expresses just what they want to say. Little by little the light will dawn for the student. The motivation will kick in. Children will feel that urgency to get it right—to work on their writing in order to produce a piece of writing that lives and breathes.

Charts

These charts may be reproduced, enlarged, or handprinted, as you wish. They can be modified and expanded. Sometimes a student with good handwriting skills can make a beautiful chart for you. It doesn't take up your time, and the child contributes to the class.

Charts are helpful because they keep all of the points that you want students to remember in full view, until students do these things automatically.

Worksheets

Feel free to use and adapt as many or as few as you need.

What Writing Partners Do

☀ Listen to others as you would like others to listen to you.

☀ Find the particular thing that you liked in someone's writing, and make a positive comment about it.

☀ Ask a question about something you didn't understand, or something you are curious about.

☀ Share with your fellow writers some suggestions you might have, but remember that they must choose what to do with their pieces.

What Writing Is Not:

* Something that you just have to get done and forget.

* An assignment that the teacher gives you.

* The same as talking.

What Writing Is:

* A chance to tell about something clearly.

* Thoughts on paper that sometimes come out quickly and easily, but usually take quite a bit of thought and rewriting.

* Words used to make sense to the reader and to stir up the reader's interest.

* A way to find out what you already know.

* A way to find out about yourself—what you think and feel.

CHART 2   99

How to Conduct a Writers' Conference:

1. Listen carefully as the child reads the piece aloud to you.

2. Comment briefly about your reaction to the piece.

3. Ask questions.

4. Help the writer to discover for himself or herself what needs to be changed in the story.

5. Before closing this conference, ask the writer what he or she plans to do with the piece.

Questions for Writers— Try Some!

1. How do you feel about your story so far?

2. Are you finished, or do you want to write more? What are you planning to write?

3. What part works the best for you? Why?

4. What part, if any, does not work for you? Do you want to get rid of it, or do you want to change it?

5. Tell me more about . . . .

6. Is there anything unusual about . . . ?

7. I don't understand what you meant when you wrote . . . .

8. Why did you choose this topic?

9. Did you say what you really wanted to in this piece?

10. Who are you writing this for? (Who is your audience?)

11. What is your purpose in writing this piece?

12. What title would you give this piece?

CHART 4   101

How to Grab the Interest of the Reader

❂ Use a lively quotation.

❂ Use dialogue.

❂ Say something unusual.

❂ Create a sense of drama.

❂ Mention a strange or interesting place.

❂ Use action words.

❂ Use exclamations.

❂ Use humor.

❂ Present a problem.

Ask These Questions to Improve Your Writing:

1. What title do I want?

2. Does my first sentence make people want to read more?

3. Is the piece about one main idea? (Is it focused?)

4. Does the writing say what I want it to say?

5. Who is going to read this? (Who is my audience?)

6. Does it make sense?

7. Does this piece fulfill the purpose I had in writing it?

8. Did I end it well?

CHART 6 *103*

Ideas for Revising

☀ Create an opening that grabs attention.

☀ Add details.

☀ Change some verbs to action verbs.

☀ Use dialogue.

☀ Show how characters feel.

☀ Organize your paragraphs.

☀ Use figurative language.

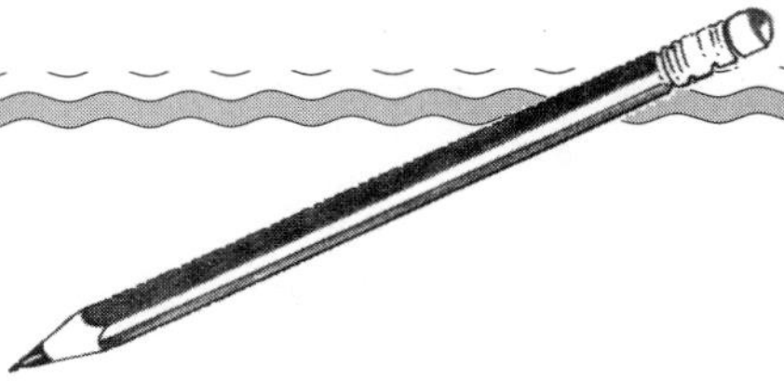

Editing Marks: # Examples:

Add a word or words   ∧

Omit a word or words   �ل

Add a period   ⊙

Add a comma   ∧

Start a new paragraph   ¶

Correct the spelling   sp. ◯

Make a capital letter   ≡

                    CHART 8   105

Name of Writer: _____

Class: _____ Date: _____

Name of Editing Partner: _____

Editing Check

Look over your final draft carefully. Using a pencil, pen, or marker different in color from what you used in the draft, mark the changes as suggested by each question below. When complete, check the box. Then give to your editing partner to check. When both checks are made, give to your teacher for final editing.

☐ ☐

Writer   **Peer Editor**

1. Are you unsure of the standard spelling of any words? Circle them and correct them by looking up the words in a dictionary.

☐ ☐

Writer   **Peer Editor**

2. Does every sentence begin with a capital letter and end with a period, question mark, or exclamation point? What about commas? Add correct punctuation.

☐ ☐

Writer   **Peer Editor**

3. Are there any long, run-on sentences? Break them up.

☐ ☐

Writer   **Peer Editor**

4. Do you have any unnecessary words? Eliminate them. Change words that are repeated unnecessarily. Are there any missing words? Add them.

Name of Writer: _____

Class: _____ Date: _____

Portfolio Criteria

Before selecting a piece of writing for your portfolio, make sure that all, or almost all, of the following is true. Place a check in those boxes:

☐   The writing piece is complete, presentable, and well organized.

☐   The writing is clear.

☐   The writing flows.

☐   The writing is appropriate for the audience.

☐   The purpose is fulfilled.

☐   The subject matter is important to the writer.

☐   Qualities of good writing are evident.

☐   The writing expresses the material creatively.

Name of Writer: _____

Class: _____ Date: _____

Student Reflection on Writing

Choose one of the topics below, or more than one, and write some of the things you've learned about writing, and some of immediate goals you have as a writer:

How I have grown as a writer:

_____

_____

_____

_____

How I have met my goals in writing:

_____

_____

_____

_____

What I need to do next:

_____

_____

_____

_____

Name of Writer: _____

Class: _____ Date: _____

Student Portfolio Reflection

Title of Piece of Writing:

_____

_____

_____

_____

_____

I chose this piece of writing for my portfolio because:

_____

_____

_____

_____

_____

_____

_____

_____

Name of Reader: _____

Name of Writer: _____

Class: _____ Date: _____

Reader's Response

Check one box:

☐ Response to the following piece of writing

☐ Response to the Portfolio

Thank you for sharing your writing with me. Here is my response:

Reactions

_____

_____

_____

_____

_____

Questions

_____

_____

_____

_____

_____

Name of Writer: _____

Class: _____ Date: _____

Writing Web

In the main oval, write your main topic. In the outer ovals, write subtopics.

A Selected Bibliography

The Art of Teaching Writing by Lucy McCormick Calkins (Heinemann, New Edition, 1994).

Best Practices by Steven Zemelman, Harvey Daniels, and Arthur Hyde (Heinemann, 1993).

Deep Revision by Meredith Sue Willis (Teachers & Writers Collaborative, 1993).

The Elements of Style by William Strunk, Jr. and E. B. White (Allyn and Bacon, Third Edition, 1979).

The Fiction Writer's Handbook by Hollie and Whit Burnett (HarperCollins, 1975).

Literacy at the Crossroads by Regie Routman (Heinemann, 1996).

Shoptalk: Learning to Write with Writers by Donald Murray (Heinemann, 1990).

Teaching Writing: A Workshop Approach by Adele Fiderer (Scholastic Professional Books, 1993).

The Writer's Art by James J. Kilpatrick (Andrews, McMeel, & Parker, 1984).

Writing: Teachers & Writers at Work by Donald H. Graves (Heinemann, 1983).

Writing to Learn by William Zinsser (HarperCollins, 1989).